Ivarna Kalinkova's

Soulmate Astrology

Volume one

Purple Inkwell Books

Dedicated to all who love,

or wish to love.

Ivarna Kalinkova's
Soulmate Astrology
Volume one

Ivarna Kalinkova

Purple Inkwell Books

Copyright © Ivarna Kalinkova 2011

All Rights Reserved

The moral right of Ivarna Kalinkova to be identified as the author of this work has been asserted by her in accordance with the Copyright, Design and Patents Act 1988

No part of this book may be reproduced or transmitted in any form or by any means, graphic, electronic, or mechanical, including photocopying, recording, taping, or by any information storage or retrieval system, without permission in writing from both the author and publisher.

While every effort has been made to ensure accuracy throughout this book errors may occur. Ivarna Kalinkova and the publisher will not be held responsible for any loss or damage suffered as a result of the information contained.

First published in Great Britain 2011 by

Purple Inkwell Books

email: editor@purpleinkwell.co.uk

internet: www.purpleinkwell.co.uk

ISBN 978-0-9567454-0-8

Soulmate Astrology by Ivarna Kalinkova was first published in Japan 2007 ISBN 978-4-8047-6149-7. This is the first English publication, updated and extended.

About the book

Ivarna developed her unique Soulmate readings over many years of birth chart analysis for clients world wide. One of her clients from Japan featured her 'Soulmate Readings' in a book a few years ago, the title translated into English reads 'Meeting your soulmate through first meeting your true self'. When asked the about the book she gave this inspiring reply;

"I wrote of my own experience with you, your Soulmate Reading, to explain that we are soul beings and we decide our life plan including soulmate before we were born. As so many women remain single nowadays in Japan worrying if they have any chance to meet their soulmate. I wanted to assure everyone has got soulmate, but it does not mean that that brings happiness, and most important thing is our spiritual growth and if we know our true desire, our true voice, we live a life which we planned beforehand to develop our spirituality and which we feel fulfilled in deepest level, and I put some exercises to find our true voice."

Since then Ivarna's popularity in Japan as grown steadily and Ivarna's unique style of interpretation now features on Japanese astrology websites and mobile phone dial-up readings.

You don't need to have a great knowledge of astrology to enjoy this book, although a little of the basics of Signs and Houses will prove useful and easy to pick up from general astrology books and websites. You can also obtain your own Natal or Birth chart online for free, details can be found at the end of the book. If you have not read a chart before make sure it has a key that shows astrological symbols and what they mean, so you can look at the chart and find the position of your planets, the signs on your houses and your ascendant.

Enjoy this book,

Ivarna Kalinkova

Contents

Introduction to Astrology — *1*
Zodiac Signs — *3*
Types of Karmic and Soulmate Bonds — *9*
Soulmate or Infatuation — *14*
Soulmate in the Making — *39*
Does Everyone Have a Soulmate. — *43*
A Sample Reading — *45*
Synastry — *53*
Loved and lost. — *56*
When A Soulmate Is Not A Soulmate. — *66*
Paths of Misdirection — *72*
Karma of Planets in the Seventh House — *74*
The Signs on the Seventh House — *79*
Karmic Cloths — *84*
Example of Karmic Synastry Question. — *86*
The Karma Explained. — *93*
The Luminaries - Moon — *97*
The Luminaries - Sun — *101*
When Will I Meet My Soulmate? — *105*
The curiosity shop — *110*

Introduction to Astrology

The stars are full of secrets. Time itself is a door. You stand on the threshold and the history of your life is written in a single instant. Everything there is to know about you, is concealed inside that one moment, invisibly like the yolk within an egg. That splinter of time is ripened by the cosmos in the way a seed is activated to grow in the heavy earth towards the yellow Sun. That moment of course is your birth time. Your character, your future your destiny and all you will ever become is encased within it . This may sound too dire, too fatalistic for those who love freedom. But fate and free will have no contradiction, they are like the Bride and Groom in an eternal cosmic marriage. Fate is not the opposite of free will, no more than night is the opposite of day. Fate is an absence of free will. The one cannot exist without the other.

It is easiest to understand the concept of astrology if you think of one cosmic mote in time as being quite separate, and unique from all the other moments. A fragment locked in time that will live, die and never come again, that has its own soul, history and feeling. Think of it as a separate solid object, imagine it as a Russian doll. The Russian doll is an apt symbol of your soul. Inside this doll is another, and another, each identical and yet unique. Like layers going back in time. Imagine each doll is a year of your life; going back to your birth. Back beyond the smallest doll to the genetic pattern it was made from. Then imagine each doll is an aspect of your character going deeper and deeper below the surface, back to its same root beginning. The layers of your character, body, mind spirit, built and rebuilt, a continuing processes one round the other as the years go on. Then think of reincarnation, each doll is a past incarnation going back beyond the other into time; but they all begin with the same tiny doll, the same small distant mote of time. Back beyond this tiniest doll some invisible pattern is set in infinity. The chart of your nativity, is the original design from which the all the Russian dolls that are you have been fashioned

It is this pattern or cosmic design that astrology interprets. It is symbolized by your chart. Your birth date, time and place. That moment of time holds the key to everything. Much in the way that an Orchid seed has the genetic pattern of the beautiful flower within, this chart holds the spiritual pattern, from which your life and destiny will grow. No two orchids are alike, no two people, or two charts are exactly alike.

An astrologer can "read" the secret cosmic code of your Natal chart and advise you. He can untangle this cloth of time and use the special psychic skills in that advice, just as a scientist uses his or her special science skills to interpret a genetic code. Or a gardener can tell you how a seedling is growing and what to do to make it grow better. Astrology is a much older science and it is more mystical or mysterious. This book is about the astrology of soulmates, it is one small branch of a vast tree.. You don't have to be an astrologer to derive something new and original from its pages, but I hope you will induced by it to be my student and to study my special form of cosmic wisdom.

Zodiac Signs

There are only twelve Zodiac signs, so any reading based on them must by necessity be very general. For each sign covers a twelfth of the population. In your own chart the degree of your zodiac sign and the astrological house it occupies, the ruling planet of that sign and any planet your Sun aspects will also add or detract something and help make the picture more individual than from these very general indications. But because everyone knows their zodiac sign, we begin this book in this simple way. Later in our soulmate journey and in the steps of this book the astrology becomes ever complex.

Aries

Born under Aries your soulmate is one who seems as though he will gain success in life. Dominant; the strong quiet one, and love is deep and impulsive, or sometimes comes after a rejection. Loss turned to victory. He is not always the first love or first choice. Your spirit dislikes being dependant or totally reliant on another. You are ambitious, and the soul mate you will desire, may be a man of substance. One who allows you to stand tall. Aries females often want to marry a man of higher position than their friends or sisters have married. Someone to raise you up when you need to hold your head high in life and win. Aries man, is masculine, and needs a feminine sort who is submissive and trusting, who will make him feel strong.

Taurus

The slow and gradual realization that someone matters

to you ever more deeply, the dawning of love, is how you will recognize your predestined partner. Your soulmate will offer security and commitment. You will be expected to accept his traditions, ways and family values. Vows that are never broken. Your soulmate will be the steady faithful type. But may also be possessive. Your soulmate is someone reliable who will always be there for you.

Gemini

Your soulmate will seem like a twin spirit, the dear friend you always wanted but much more wonderful than any friend you have known. It is difficult for you to find all you need in just one person. Like an ever changing flame, your soulmate can seem one thing then another, a partner who is entertaining clever and bright, who can adapt to the changing times in your life. There is something of the youth in this person, and no matter how many times you have loved before, this love is fresh and new.

Cancer

Someone you can trust, who will cherish and care for you. This may be a provider materially or spiritually. The soulmate has a sensitive vulnerable side, or something that reflects the child inside of you and brings out your care taker instincts. A partner who feels familiar like one of the family, who is your rock, someone you will cling to like a shadow. A tender sympathetic soul who copes with your vulnerability or moodiness and who likes being looked after as much as you.

Leo

Your soulmate is dazzling and dramatic someone whom you can feel very proud to know. A talented and much admired man, who has chosen you amongst all others. You shine in his reflected light. A relationship that is uplifting, prestigious, and which other people will admire and recognize. A film star or royal charisma. A man who will make grand generous gestures of love and who will give a lot of attention and affection. And you alone in the entire world will understand him and see the insecurity beneath the confident sparkling surface.

Virgo

You offer unconditional love, to just one love. No other man can move you deeply but him. So you acquiesce too much and your predestined partner doesn't know where the line is drawn. You try to be the perfect partner. Your soulmate will be a much Admired, strong masculine, rugged warm witty clever cool dignified and earthy with a good physique. One who lives life and love by his own set of rules. Slow to commit to you but an enduring love..

Libra

Your soulmate is attractive, romantic, refined in manners, and well dressed. A relationship with a touch of luxury or class and romance about it. Desire for peace a fear of rejection. This sign puts up with a lot in life, loyal, dutiful devoted. You do not want to be independent. You want to be cherished and provided for. A relationship that will last for life, built round duty respect loyalty and devotion.

Scorpio.

Born under Scorpio, your soulmate is mysterious, impenetrable and has hidden powers. You seek something not ordinary. A power some people find scary. Refinement. You also want someone of interesting mentality, who can hold your attention and captivate you. Scorpio relationships often have a hidden kind of love. The soulmate may be a secret, or love may never be spoken of between you, relationship that has its share of walking in darkness but is immensely powerful and will transform you as a person, or transform your life totally.

Sagittarius

Your soulmate will take your heart by storm. He will be protective. Reliably and sturdy, Fit and healthy and will look it. An honest man, a pillar of the community, good at heart and sturdy in soul. He can bring the light of cheer and enthusiasm into your gloom, and brighten you darkest moment. A little possessive perhaps, but dependable, faithful and one who is a success in his own life and profusion.. You will be honest and open with each other.

Capricorn

Your soulmate is self disciplined, controlled and knows what he wants in life. A man you will first respect and then love, afraid that he will hurt you, you are restrained. He is restrained and afraid you will break his heart. It is a working relationship. Practical, feet on the ground, Loyal a help mate as well as a soulmate. At times it will seem to lack romance, but there is a passionate earthy core. Your predestined partner will offer strong support worldly support a relationship over shadowed by many things, every day things, work, sorrows, but through it all duty loyalty. Mutual co operation..

Aquarius

This man will inspire you, an unusual soulmate, cool, modern, someone whose intellect and taste appeals to you. He will intrigue and excite you mentally. A man of intelligence and independence. A relationship that is held lightly, loosely at first, like a friendship. Love unspoken. Much detachment. Unusual or unconventional soulmate. The sort of person, or kind of relationship that you never really envisaged or imagined for yourself, but who seems destined. A love that just happens like a storm in summer and builds its own momentum. A relationship full of chance elements and coincidence.

Pisces.

Strong, moody, capable but dreamy. Someone who's deep inner worth you can see, even when others cannot. Someone you'd never abandon. Sensitive stormy, tempestuous. The relationship with your soulmate can be changeable and may involve some emotional or spiritual sacrifice. Something you have to give up to get him. The negative side of this sign can bring 'Victim Savior' relationships, co-dependant relationships. Addictive relationships and suffering. The positive side spiritual or artistic relationships that heal something within you, relationship that some creative venture will come out of, but which you have to give your life to. Life long devotion.

Astrology is about fate and predestination. But it is also about making your own fate. There is nothing mysterious about prediction. The present circumstances are a result of the past ones that lead up to it. From the present we can predict the future outcome. Equally we can work with the present and the outcomes of the past to change the "future" slightly to improve our lives, and to lead us to a love that will transform our life. A love like no other has ever been..

You can find more basics of astrology at Ivarna's website: www.Ivarna.com.

Types of Karmic and Soulmate Bonds

Soulmate

The true definition of a Soulmate is someone who has always loved you, whose spirit has been irresistibly attracted to yours from the beginning of time, whom you may have met before, time and time in past lives, or may be meeting for the first time. A predestined lover. One who has been brought to the fatalistic point in history where your two pre destined paths must merge so that you can complete your destiny. Such a bond creates an intense and overpowering love.

This is the kind of relationship that I am asked most often to predict in the astrology readings. The great love relationship, that comes perhaps only once in a life time. The love that transforms us. If we are very lucky we may meet a second soulmate, but such relationship are rarer.

Soulmate of course is a convenient word, used as a general term and so it can have many definitions depending on who is saying the word. Like the term " Girl Friend " it has a whole larder of uses. If a lesbian refers to her girlfriend, we know it generally imply something different to when a heterosexual woman talks brightly of her girl friend!. When a man uses the term it can mean anything from someone he is dating, to someone he has lived with for the past decade. Soulmate is used in the same diverse way. I do not think that exact definitions are so important, but they are included in this book because people do ask.

Twin Souls

Some people believe that when our soul and spirit was created, before time began, and before we walked the earth, the essence or substance of our soul and spirit was split into pieces, like identical embryos in the mother's womb, but our womb was time and space and whatever existed between worlds.

A twin soul of which we may have many is the same essence as us on a very deep level but also uniquely different. There is the theory that mankind is lonely and the sex urge is a subconscious attempt to reuniting these half's to become one again, which is why if a soulmate or twin soul is of the appropriate sex and right age there is an irresistible attraction. A twin soul is literally our "other half ". If we meet a twin soul it is a rare relationship. And it isn't always a romantic one. A twin soul can be a person of either sex, any age, it can even be a figure from history, or someone we have never met, but who we seem to have so much in common with we instinctively feel we are them, or were them in another life, or that we should have known them, as friend or lover.. When twin souls meet up, regardless of whether they are best friend, or lovers, or family members, they are usually inseparable, and so are often called soulmates. A Soulmate can be a twin soul but it isn't always.

If you think of our human as a Russian doll with many layers of mind and spirit and soul within it, one inside the other The soul is simply a deeper layer, of us than the spirit. The links between souls are deeper than those between spirits. But when the soul's essence is divide into two (or more), the spirits essence the next layer down automatically is divided too.. If it didn't, you get a unique situation where two people, two souls, shared a common mind, total telepathy. There are legends about such people or races. If the spirits essence doesn't divide fully, you get fragments of telepathy but not total between twin souls.

A twin soul is always also a twin spirit. So the terms are used interchangeably. (Though confusingly a twin spirit isn't always a twin soul)

A twin soul is created of the same spiritual essence, like a twin. But usually there are elements of reversal, so that the Twin, may have some opposite quality we lack, or may have a strength where we have a weakness. And we may have some quality the twin lacks. But in other ways very similar. A twin spirit can be the same sex, or the opposite sex, so when you meet a twin spirit you don't necessity meet a soulmate in the usual sense or a lover but you can do. What you meet in twin soul is someone who will bring enlightenment. I don't think enlightenment *has* to come through someone else's magnetism, but it helps. Like a fusion. The two half's, If say an artist meets their twin soul, to work on the same project, they may love or hate that person, but they will do their best work with them, as though meeting the twin soul has unlocked something, or given them a greater power. Each twin benefits.

On rare occasions you get a twin soul, where one is good, the other evil. In literature and great books of the past the hero and the anti hero are often symbolic of twin souls, one good, one bad, but both equal in their power. In real life it is not usually that clear cut, but if one twin has elements of bad in the character and the other good, or one has all the strength, the other all the weakens their meeting is one where they will either reform each other or destroy each other. Opposites are the same in the end. It is quite rare to meet a twin soul. But I believe we probably have several "twins", more so if someone has an important destiny, the twins are then like reserve players in a game, a game of destiny, so that if that person fails or faulters on destiny's path, one of the other twins can be called by fate to carry in that "important" destiny.

What to look for in the chart

Astrological clues; Mercury Venus conjunctions in the chart; Also the Sun conjunct either of these planets. Venus in Gemini, the person is sure to meet a twin soul; these planets in the third or ninth house of a natal chart often suggest that a twin soul has incarnated on earth in this same era as you, and you will one day come into contact with this twin. Gemini rising, or Mercury rising; Saturn conjunct with Venus, Sun or mercury, means life may be difficult but there will eventually be a supportive twin soul, to lighten the load, and often older. Synastry aspects between two peoples chart along these same suggestions, may point to the two being twin souls, or twin spirits)

Twin Spirit.

Following the ancient myth that when the soul substance or essence incarnates each soul sibling becomes lost to the other and follows a different human path. The different destiny of the people with the same soul essences will shape or mould the spirit within that destiny, life after life. It makes us what we are. A twin spirit can simply be someone whose spirit has made or has shaped itself in a similar pattern to yours, like two rare birds, which are not directly related but are of the same breed. When an encounter occurs there is an affinity.

Like a nest of birds from the same batch of eggs, a twin spirit can also be a twin soul, and a soulmate, right down the line, but not always. Two birds from two entirely isolated nests can be identical too, they can be twin spirits without being twin souls, or soulmates. The relationship diminishes like the Russian doll as we go down the layers, from soul to spirit to mind. In our life time we are fortune if we meet any one of the other. Few people meet both. In some ways it is also definition of words, as some people use these terms inter changeably, less exactly to mean different things. Just as some people may use the word soulmate more casualty to refer to any lover, husband, or partner who seems lasting and right.

What to look for in the chart
Astrological clues; Mercury Venus conjunctions in the chart; Also the Sun or Moon conjunct either of these planets. Venus in Gemini, synastry connections between Venus and mercury. These planets in the third or ninth house of a natal chart often suggest that a twin spirit, you will one day come into contact with this twin. Gemini rising, or Mercury rising; Saturn conjunct with Venus, Sun or mercury

A Spiritual twin;
Someone who is not necessarily our own soul essence, but someone very like us in spirit. The term again. Like

twin spirit, is often used in a casual lighter less deep way, to describe someone we have a lot in common with. They may share our faith, our ideals and our motivations and mentality. That is to say their spirit is like ours, or even linked to ours in some mysterious way, but their soul or deeper essence that goes back to creation is not.. A twin spirit is usually means more to us than a spiritual twin, (because it may have the same essence). With a spiritual twin the relationship is often less close or intense, it can be more transient and describes a relationship that is purely spiritual, or intellectual, a relationship the mind, and character, rather than romantic, or sexual. But there is always an affinity. Spiritual twins always share something that unites them, say the same beliefs, or higher motivation or studies, or same aims and task in life. It is a common relationship in what is often termed "business soulmates". They are like two friends linked to a common purpose, but tend to have quite separate lives too.

So many terms are used in a lighter less deep sense, to describe someone we have a lot in common with. It is confusing to use both words casually and correctly to mean the same thing, but definitions are theoretical they may raise the mind to contemplate at a higher level, but it is in the practical world that relationships take place..

Soulmate or Infatuation

A soulmate is someone who shares the design of our future destiny. A soul that merges with us. Ones whose life or fate is inexorably connected with ours through out eternity, and who possess what we lack. Or has the tools to help us do our predestined chore. As though we hold part of the picture of a fate or one part of the jigsaw and he holds the other part, when the two pieces come together a new picture emerges that could not be seen before. This image is of a future destiny. We don't always love a twin spirit, or twin soul in the romantic sense. But with a soulmate there is always love, a deep compelling endless love that feels like nothing on earth.

The soulmate strikes straight at the heart when we meet, like reflection of all we have every subconsciously wanted in a man or woman. He can carry elements of our twin soul in his character, elements of our self, our teacher, father, or mother, Guardian, our highest hopes our deepest fears, they are all mingled, because they are all a reflection of what we love and a reflection of him, and he is the reflection of them. It is a person who carries our true "anima", and true destiny. We carry the soulmates imprint inside of us in the same way, like a piece of life's puzzle and when we meet, this anima and animus matches exactly like a lock and a key, and we are magnetized by it, inseparably drawn and held. It unlocks the door of a destiny that we cannot find on our own. Sometimes it opens other psychic channels too, past lives, telepathy. A new purpose. A soulmate is a special love. It is the fusion of the true anima and animus, It is also a creative flow, like a river of time that can transform our lives beautifully and totally over a era of months or years, into something much better.

For those on a purely ordinary human level without creative power, or psychic purpose, this creative flow, is physical and is diverted into sex, the worldly task of being together, children, home making and all that these things entail. For others life finds a new sense of direction and purpose, the transforming creativity is channeled towards creative project, or some spiritual aim. A life's work, or a Healing power, in your own or other peoples lives, an important task to complete in the world. Soulmates come together for a uniquely important purpose, as well as the unusual special love that only that person can give.

It is a mystical and romantic attraction that transcends every day reality. The sort of relationship that passionate mysterious love affairs are made of. But it is more complicated than that. I think we sometimes live in many realities at the same time, one wrapped within the other again like the Russian doll. The present moment and the past lives overlap a little. That soulmate relationships triggers memories, like a semi transparent cloth, even though you cannot consciously reach it the dim color of former live filters through. There are times in life when the veil between this solid world and the psychic is very thin and we get insights, intuitions, unrecognized memories and deep compelling loves and vision of the future. The soulmate experience is one such love.

Infatuation the Dark Side of the Soulmate Path.

How do you tell the difference?. An infatuation is an involvement with suffering. Not an involvement with a soulmate, but it sometimes takes hindsight to tell the difference. An infatuation is one of loves paths of misdirection, the commonest road. But has a value, it is also called Anima projection.

Anima Projection

Some lovers have a mesmerizing emotional effect. You encounter them and from that day forward you are never free of them. You become obsessed. Like a shadow of illusion falling over your life and obscuring the sharpness or hardness of reality. Your mind is always chained to that person, in idle moments it fills up your dreams, it permeates you thoughts. This can happen even if you have barely spoken a word to him. Or it can happen when you meet and become lovers, and may not even like each other but there's a compelling attraction, a love that will not let you go. Or a turbulent relationship, that you cannot leave. Someone who you cannot live with, but cannot live without. Infatuation is an addictive lingering desire. Life can seem threadbare without it, even though it brings desperation, and pain. But unlike the soulmate union, the desperation doesn't resolve. It has no happy ending, you walk through it bare foot on the thorny road of love and are left cut and bleeding. Unlike a real soulmate, we don't find our anima in this love, we find a mirage, when we reach for it, it is not real, and it is a spellbinding illusion. In ages past it was called simply "Fascination". The relationship ends but for you it never does. You leave, you return, you cannot let go, even though you know it ends again, even though you know he will hurt you again in the same way, your mind is trapped and you are a prisoner. This is what is known as Anima projection. The man is a reflection of your anima.

Most people go through life and never encounter the phenomena of anima projection, just as most people cross through a desert and never see a mirage.

Astrologically when it's an anima projection not a true soulmate. One of two things may happen. There can either be a curious lack of aspects between the charts, only tenuous links, minor aspects, as though nothing bonds the two people together, this shows that the relationship is as flimsy as a dream, that it can have no substance. The astrologers task is then to take the strongest aspect, as this is like the amber that holds the fly in a death grip, or the pin through an ornamental butterfly, it symbolizes the illusion that pins the victim to the dream. By careful analysis you can free the person. But only if they are willing to be free, for false love like all addictions can only be relinquished willingly. The second scenario is that there can be many difficult chart connections between the two people's charts. As difficult as the relationship itself, but there will be no soulmate aspects. A relationship with a true soulmate may not always be idyllic, but it teaches you what you need to know about yourself, to find completeness. If you are in denial about what you need to know, you may not like what you have to face. Through love relationships, and misplaced love like Infatuations, you have the opportunity to face yourself and do something about it.

The following planets are often heavily involved in anima projection/ infatuations.

Pluto; since in mythology he is god of the underworld, the dark or hidden side of the subconscious, and the things you have denied in yourself. Pluto rules obsessions, secret or hidden passions, and Anima projection is secret and subconscious since it involves only the self and an illusion.

Venus; conjunctions and oppositions in a synastry between two people's charts can be suspect. As can Pluto Moon and Neptune aspects.

Neptune; the planet of illusion is also often involved, with love planets, like Venus, showing the illusion of love. Neptune in the seventh house, sometimes shows the person has the potential for illusion or self deception, this is stronger still if the ruling planet of the ascendant is in conjunction with Neptune, because

Neptune can be illusions, the ascendant is the self, and the ruler with Neptune the tendency to delude oneself, in the seventh house, the self deception is about the lover, marriage or relationships. Though as always it depends on the rest of the chart..

There are complex patterns in advanced astrology but the above are just a few clues, a few starting points for those studying basic astrology.

For those not involved with astrology I will explain what an anima is, it is believed in Jungian psychology that in the mind of every man there is an ideal women, she is composed of the feminine elements and characteristics of himself that he has repressed being a man. This ideal woman is subconscious, the conscious mind doesn't recognize it, not even as a dream or fantasy. Over the years things he desires or admires in a woman get added together to form this subconscious ghost picture. Usually the way she looks, a certain expression, a certain gesture, all the subtle nuances that he admires or which has deeper meaning for him. He may add some subtle things from film stars he admires. He may have repressed his admiration for these stars, thinking it unmanly, fragments of former lovers, or some unrecognized characteristic of his mother, say her kindness, or his brothers boyish camaraderie. Again all repressed in the light of day, because we are not supposed to find our mothers or brothers attractive. Many things as a man grows up go to make this subconscious picture. Over the years it changes with his experience of life. He is unaware he carries this picture, it's not like a photo in his wallet. But when he meets a woman who has one or two characteristics that resemble this subconscious portrait, he imagines that she also possess all the other things he desires, even if these desires are so deep he cannot name them or recognize what they are, things lost in the depth of time, but he blinds himself to the real women, seeing only his dream which he falls deeply in love with. He is like a drowning man who cannot be rescued.

Think of the projection like the projection of a film onto a blank wall, an image of a lovely woman. But this image is projected not onto a wall but into another person. He becomes obsessed, infatuated, even if he wants to be free of it, he cannot, it's irresistible like an assault from the unconscious mind that he has no control over he is compelled to fall in love. This is called animus projection. A woman has in her subconscious a kind of unknown man, a stranger who is composed of all the masculine things she has repressed or buried and again when she meets a man who has some characteristic again she can project the whole of the rest onto him. This is called Anima projection.

An anima is something inside of us like a hidden image that we project onto the man we meet, again like projecting a film onto a wall, so we see only that illusion and not the real person. The man is always somewhat like the image of course or we wouldn't project it; but he is also different, and so the relationship is destined to be tragically unhappy or unrequited, or doomed not to last.

If it happens once or twice and mildly it is just a beautiful infatuation and usually we recognize it as such, and walk on eventually. But if it happens deeply it is mistaken for love, and feels like it, every bit as wonderful every bit as tormenting painful. Now some people with this mental make up project the inner dream onto all potential partners, and they cant see the real person they are courting, only the figure they want to see in him or her, this is very common, consequently the relationship always begins like the romance of the century, and ends disappointingly when the person they have become infatuated with either breaks it off because he feels you are not seeing him or understanding him or relating to him a the person he is.

Or else the relationship fails of its own accord because the mans own strong character breaks through your illusion, and shatters it to pieces to the point when you can no longer deceive yourself about him, He becomes a the real person whom he always was. The real person might be cruel selfish, hard, nothing like the fake image you love. The dream no longer covers the cracks in the image, the blindness falls from your eyes you are forced to see this person as he is, with all his faults, and imperfections, there is an immense short fall. You feel disappointed, badly let down, hurt, but that pain is just the blow of seeing the truth devoid of the dream.

It can form a psychological pattern relationship after

relationship that always ends the same way in disappointment and despair. Making every step of life painful and lonely. So that when that happens, you fall in and out of love. And are subconsciously driven to look for the next person to throw this same illusion or image over, to have some relief from the pain and loneliness and to feel; the ecstasy of this dream love again wrap round us like a velvet cape to smother the pain, to douse it in dreams of romance. A life becomes a series of compelling addictive infatuations that are like dope to an unhappy soul.

Let me make it clear, when we seek our soulmate we seek our Anima. The path of misdirection here is not that we seek the Anima, but that we project an image of it onto some who does not possess the qualities of our Anima. Then fall in love with the image and become imprisoned by it. What we love is not the real person, not even the real Anima.

The Moon is the actual anima or animus. In astrology the Sun represents ourselves and the Moon is our shadow, our anima. The Sun is the day, the conscious self, the whole self, the Moon is the night the dark unconscious. Sun and Moon aspects linked with anima projection aspects in synastry charts, can mean it is not an illusion but the true anima.

In a soulmate's chart and your own there are always many links that form a destiny. I often get people who are infatuated, smitten sometimes with quite ordinary people, People at work who never speak to them for example, people they barely know, but hope to know, the face in the crowd. When the two charts are compared usually there is maybe only one tied aspects and nothing else, if no aspects exist no future exists, and its possible to say to the person, This is a infatuation, and I think it happened because he remained you of someone, or because your subconscious badly needs love and is misinterpreting what this man really means in your life. Or whatever the chart happens to reveal about the infatuation in the link it has with the other chart. All charts are individual and different so are all synastry.

In most anima projections, a relationship does exist between the two people, they are not stars that one glimpses in the night sky that fade in a moment and are gone, not faces that smile in a crowd, and so because a relationship of sorts exists there are usually a feast of aspects in the synastry chart that outlines the problem, and aspects within the Natal chart which overlap the synastry and reveal the one sidedness of the affections. The other differences between that and a soulmate chart are while the soulmate chart may outline problems too, it will show feelings and the attachment being reciprocated, it will sketch out a future, the planets will not be shrouded by aspects of illusion.

Repeated infatuation;. Astrologically, a planet close to the Sun in a Natal chart tends towards obsession. If this conjuncting planet, and please note it's the planet not the Sun itself, that produces obsession interests, if this planet is linked in some way with the seventh house, its ruler, or with Mars or Venus, it can point to a pattern of obsession, in the Natal chart. Obsession and infatuation are not always the same things. A person can be obsessed with love in other ways, it is not infatuation that induces obsession. There is for instance irrational jealousy that borders on obsession but if the propensity is there in the chart, it is a step closer to infatuation occurring.

Neptune is the lord of illusion when he is strong in a natal chart it is easy too delude oneself . Neptune , aspecting the Moon, makes the Moon become the Mistress of illusion in certain positions, the purveyor of false hope. The Moon is the true anima, but Neptune leads it astray, disguises or fools you into thinking someone as the true Anima. Venus opposition Neptune or conjunct Neptune, symbolizes loves delusion and square Pluto in the Natal chart will show an addictive personality, the potential to weave a garment of desire and fascination into a fake picture of love. But always it shows only a potential. Always the aspects are suspects, not certainties. When these aspects in the natal chart link to planets of romance and delusion in a synastry, one has to be very careful in interpreting the synastry. For even if the love is not false the client will labor under some illusion regarding the relationship.

The same conclusion comes where these natal aspects exist and where there are no synastry aspects. False love and projection, unreciprocated feelings can be suspected then. But there must always be a caution, just as a wonderful work of art can look like an imitation, and a forgery look like a great work of art, so the chart of love and the chart of loves forgery may easily be mistaken.

More clues -. Natal Moon in Pisces, or Aries are slightly more prone to obsession love, as are Sun in Leo, Aries , Virgo, also these signs on seventh house.

In synastry, Neptune aspects between charts or strong

in the natal chart, but without many of the other chart connections to bind the charts together, can show a tendency to infatuation, though Neptune can rule foreigners too, so the Astrologer must be careful not to interpret say Neptune in the seventh house as illusion when it may simply mean an involvement to a foreigner or a liaison that is long and requires waiting for some other delays to pass. The whole chart must be considered. Venus in the twelfth house, the person may be prone to infatuations or secret dreams of love. Remember each chart is individual, and other aspects may contradict, it is the job of the astrologer to decide, there are just clues.

How to Resolve Infatuation

What can be done ? It is very difficult and requires a lot of introspection to resolve and understand. Infatuation is so seductive that the person may not want to be rescued. Life is an emptier cold place when the dream is gone. It is a desert when the pain is gone. The first step is to want to be free of the obsession. Until you truly want to be free there is no help. But Remember when you are free, you are free to meet your soulmate. To have the paradise you tasted in this mere reflection of love made real, without the agony.

To overcome anima projection; the thing is to understand that what you project or see in the other person, and love is really a part of your self that has had no outlet. You have to allow it into your life and character, so that it merges with you, you will then stop seeking it in other people and the love you will find when you next love will be real and true. The difficulty is in determining which parts of you the anima represents. It is never easy or straightforward. If you find this part or characteristics in yourself and integrated it into your life, you will no longer look for it outside and be drawn into painful infatuations, the next love will be real. It requires a lot of thought to identify exactly what it is your projecting and why. And it's something that only you can know.

How to counter it; you need to look deeply at the self. A soulmate provides the missing parts of us. He provides the things we need to evolve. The tools of destiny. An infatuation does not provide these things, an infatuation is telling you that you must try to provide these things for yourself. In so doing we will be free of the infatuation, free to find a true soulmate, a relationship that will feel as deep but will be happy. For example who does this person make you " be"? What illusion is this person feeding? If the Lover makes you feel important. When the world makes you feel as if you are a person of no consequence. Then what you have to find is the value within yourself. The sense of self importance. If you feel strong enough to face life so long as you have this person, you have to find inner strength, not strength from him. To do so you have to analyze past situations where you have been made to feel unimportant, or humiliated, or worthless and heal them, you have to recognize your strengths and bring them out. Try looking at situations in your life that happened up to a year before the first infatuation. The root is not always in childhood, but it is always before the infatuation. Then go back further and see if the person you're strung up on reminds you of anyone in the further past.

Clues in the chart; Saturn strongly placed; inferiority, self worth. A need to feel valuable. Neptune; persecution, rejection, weakness, escape, someone to rescue you from a situation or whole life which you're too weak and dependant to be master of. Pluto; new life, new start, Pluto may offer you a solution, a new life that you don't have the courage to carve out alone, for example the will to leave the husband, the mother, the home town, the belief that if you do, the new life will be wonderful not terrible, also a need to absolve the guilt that goes with such decision. The real soulmate will help you do so, the reflection will give only the illusion. He will seem to promise that this can be, even if he has made no solid promise. And half is in your mind but is like a reflection in a stream, never delivers that promise.

Eventually infatuation turns to its opposite, to disenchantment. Where it gave hope, it brings despair, where it make you feel valuable and cherished it makes you feel trashed and worthless. The illusion ends. Work on the psychological side of the damage, and when the work is complete next time when love unfolds its wings across your life and embraces you into shadow, the real Soulmate will be waiting there. If you go half way to meeting something, it comes half way to you., the end of illusion is only the beginning of a reality.

Karmic work is usual a little painful but rewards are great and they come in this lifetime as well as in future lives. This is the way to transform your life from hell to heaven and in the fog and dark anxiety the real soulmate will emerge a lonely figure on the path to light the lamp of destiny, and take your hand in his, and rub away all the scars of life, all the past hurts and struggles.

I am indebted to one of my clients for this question "can an infatuation ever be a true soulmate? And by working on it can it be changed to happen", like turning over a photograph from the negative to positive? The answer is yes sometimes on rare occasion it is both, like lessons that have to be learned, before we find the final happiness, astrologically in such cases the chart will usually show both soulmate aspects and infatuation aspects. Not just one or the other.

But if you are to change the pattern completely you must find it by looking dispassionately at your own life. I will give you an example, my client was a refined, genteel lady. Well brought up but in a narrow prudish, class conscious background. The men she fell for seemed to be the opposite, often rough lower class backgrounds, who were uncouth, vulgar, treated her badly, used her only for sex but who'd made a name for themselves or climbed the success ladder. These men had a degree of local fame. Small town mafia types. The occasional hard rock, coke addict musician. The local rugby star, famous for his pub brawls. We worked out that because of her background she had always had to repress her anger, repress her sexual drives, and be polite, always be the lady. She had to deny always the baser side of her own nature. We all have sexual urges, we all have angers, but she was never allowed to have these things. As a child she never been allowed to play rough or vigorous games, she always had to keep her nice dress clean, never scuff her shoes, behave with decorum, stop flinging her arms and legs about. Don't shout. Don't run

Even though she was a physically healthy energetic

little girl and a robust adult who would have enjoyed sport. She had to be moral, upright and a credit to her parents. She was also not allowed to be competitive, to work even, it was considered unladylike in her background. In some ways she had never been recognized as the person she was. Hence the attraction to men who had some small fame or recognition in their own circle, but whose fame was mingled with the dark and discredited kind, the shadow side of her own uprightness and virtue, the opposite. Opposition is rebellion. As adults we rebel against our childhood long after we should have grown up.

What she saw in these rough types, was not their roughness or uncouthness which she equated with manliness but half hated, but a freedom they had that she'd never had to express herself to be competitive, to be sexual, strong, active, dirty. To drink like a fish, to laugh like a lion. To slap another girl in the face instead of bite down her anger. To dance to life's heady mad violins, to live. Her life has been like a dress rehearsal for living, like a straight jacket of decorum that crushed all impulsiveness. She was robust, healthy, with natural drives but she had always had to play the languid repining, aloof lady in a flowered white dress and Ascot hat, standing on the sidelines of life. She had become the role she was cast in as a child and the woman she was expected to be. So this anima, this inner man was all these things, he was her shadow her dark side and he was competitive, vital, recognized, unfettered. Hence she sought this type in a lover, but met with unhappiness, because their life and hers was not at all compatible, as different as chalk from cheese.

Once she realized this, she set about to be herself, to say what she really thought more often, but naturally in a polite way that suited her walk of life, to have the freedom of speech and vitality and emotions her lovers had, without the vulgarity. She allowed the competitive side out, took up. Dressage and horse riding a sport again suited to her way of life, she felt she would like a job and prospects, the raw independence of living a less cosseted life than with her parents. Slowly she began to recognize other things, and connected bit by bit with this anima, this part of herself that she'd always repressed. She did not turn to the bad . Her new found strengths were not the toughness of the ghetto. Neither did she give into drink or drugs, which are weakness not strength. She did not emulate the anima, she found her own strength and love of life and lived it to the full in her own way. In short she became more whole through this process. As she did so the painful infatuations stopped, the type of men she was drawn to were no longer violent, drug crazed lovers or ones who made use of her for sex and nothing else. They were still tough, hard headed successful masculine types, but on her own level of life, the relationships became mutual and she married a Cricketer. He had wealth and a small amount of renown, a man who stood tall in the community. She changed her fate over a number of years by changing herself. She met the real soulmate instead of the shadow. This is a long difficult process. But the more you work on the symbols of illusion and ponder it, and think how these men reflect some hidden part of yourself, however different they seem to be from you, the more your pattern will change.

If the infatuation proves intractable, and the chart aspects are other than the ones we have outlined, you must delve to uncover a different source of illusion, not all infatuation are anima projection.

The blanket of illusion can be woven for a definite and proper purpose. In little dozes, like day dreams, it can be a mental sedative for the tormented mind, or the person so damage by life as to need a temporary refuge. There are times when we are either not strong enough or nor self understanding enough to face the truth and tackle its consequences. Some infatuation for example begins on the rebound, when a dearly held love has ended. Be gentle when you tread on illusions, you tread on dreams and they will yield in time. Even if nothing is ever done to remedy the infatuation, the strongest delusion will dissolve in time. If you're trapped by a dream and you don't want to be, don't despair, time is the healer. In other volumes in this series of books, we explore various forms of fascination. The reason this one is in our first book, is it is the more common by which we lead ourselves astray blindly stumble into the quagmire sorrows.

Karma

If you were murdered in a past life and you suddenly came face to face with someone unexpectedly who *looked* just like the killer, even though you would never have consciously known your killer, or known you were done to death, your soul would freeze for a moment in time. Your blood would run cold, with a nameless shuddering fear, then it would pass, and you wouldn't know why. There would seem no explanation and you'd never again feel anything as deep. It could be like that. If you see someone and your flesh creeps as if you'd beheld an insect or something you hold I horror, then you have met that person before in a past incarnation. If you loved a man very deeply in past lives, and saw someone just like him,. You'd react with the same love feeling. It is the past, brought to life as well as the present. It's rather like suddenly seeing the double of a lover who you didn't want to leave, or a famous person you admire walk down a street towards you, you are stunned, it shocks the spirit momentarily, it cuts through time, and then life moves on. But with a soulmate from another life it is more then momentary, the spirit feels totally compelled. It has to investigate to find out more, to walk this path again, to get to know the person, it seeks an answer to its mystery, it finds a love.

Astrological clues; scattered in this book are various karmic aspects and situations to look for. In synastry eighth house aspects suggest a relationship is from a previous incarnation. Someone's Venus or Moon or Sun in your eighth house, suggests you have met before. The ruler of your seventh house in their eighth and visa versa, you may have been married in a past life. One of the other books in this series will look in a more detailed way at karma . I can recommend it to help you understand yourself.

Karmic Relationships

Most Soulmate relationships are Karmic, But Karmic relationships can be of other sorts too. They can be with people other than the soulmate, and may involve love, or hate, friend or enemy. A person who arouses intense feelings almost from meeting, but with whom the relationship may be painful or difficult. This is because there is something left unfinished with from a past life. The purpose of such a meeting, is to settle the past. Once the karma is worked through both people are free of the painful compelling bond. They are free to choose to remain together or to part, and whichever is chosen it will feel right and happy so long as the past life karma has been resolved.

Astrological clues; aspects between the Luna nodes of one persons chart and another, show karma, also eighth house cross aspects. The complexity of the aspects and the planets involved will show the details and types of the karma. An interesting sample reading is given late in the book

Natal chart; A person born with Venus, or the ruler of the seventh house conjunct their Luna nodes axis, will almost certainly find a karmic love and soulmate that is predestined.

The elements.

The elements in the chart, earth, air, fire and water, correspond to elements within our character. In the soulmate or relationship charts, the signs and elements on the seventh house, and in the house which holds Venus, or the seventh ruler can reveal a little

Water signs symbolize the completion of things or the things that need to be completed in the relationship, old unfinished past life Karma;, Missing elements of life, things needed for Self awareness, spiritual aspects of a relationship and so on.. The pain created in the relationship in this incarnation.

So if you have Venus in a water sign, you may have to work on the love and emotion and missing spiritual of the relationship. If a water sign is on the seventh there may be incomplete karma and so on.

The earths sign, the material aspects, background and environment of the relationship in the present incarnation.

The air signs the attachments and bonds made in the relationship.

The fire signs, are the "action" in the relationship, what it will achieve in this life; what new interest and projects it may bring into its karma, to continue in future lives. The relationships potential.

ARIES, this is the way to read the signs round your Natal chart. Aries is the beginning of the zodiac, and symbolizes new interests and new karma you and your soulmate will begin together;

The house on which Aries and its ruler Mars falls in your chart gives an indication of the type of new directions. If for example Mars is in an air sign, you will generate many new and interesting ideas together, your original thinking together will create a stir, and if Aries is in the sixth house, this new way of looking at things will be applied to your health or to your working life. You may influence the way he looks after his health or thinks about fitness. He may inspire you with new thoughts about your approach to your working life, or visa versa, but together these will be the areas of the future that you'll build new beginnings on, and be ambitious about. If the Aries house in your chart is not particularly significant or connected by aspects, planets in it, to the Soulmate significator, then this influence will still be correct but it will be a less important background part of the relationship, than say if a planet in your seventh house, aspected the cusp of the Aries house, or if Venus was in Aries, or if Mars aspected the seventh. If the Aries house was not strengthened by these things, then the new directions and idea in health and work would only be a small part of the relationship, where if it was strongly reinforced by planets and aspects, it would be a dominant or major part in your future together.

All the signs can be read in a similar way,

TAURUS, The way you will Protect and. Preserve, or make secure the love.. All that keeps and strengthens in the relationship.

GEMINI, The similarities between you and the soulmate within the relationship. Unity

CANCER, The family and social circle you will make. The things that need to be developed, nurtured or matured..

LEO, what the relationship creates or produces . Art, Children, creativity. What you will show off to the world about.

VIRGO, what remains as it was before the marriage or relationship. Analysis and discrimination.

LIBRA. The ability to cooperate with the soulmate. To work together for the common good of the relationship

SCORPIO, Things hidden submerged or obscured in the relationship.

SAGITTARIUS. Things that need to be increased.

CAPRICORN, Limitations that the relationship must endure or overcome. The things that will improve with time.

AQUARIUS, Mutual intelectual attunes and interests, the motives that are common to both you and the soulmate Progressiveness and future, the way you and the soulmate will be independent from your peers.

PISCES, The things emotionally, physically spiritually that must be left behind, if the relationship is to survive and move forwards. Rebirth, future karma.

The Future

I see your face in every picture

Psychic visions are sometimes like things seen dimly in a glass. One client told me that she thought all her past loves, right form the TV character she first had a school girl crush on at twelve years old, through to the man she'd lost her virginity to at seventeen, to her two serious boyfriends, and her unorthodox lover at a foreign university she'd attended, were all like reflections of the present Soulmate love, the man she had eventually met and moved in with. She could see his character in someone, his eyes in some one else. His foreign accent in another.

This guy she loved at 12 was an actor who played some kind of time traveler who wore a black cape, the characters name was Adam, and it was the character

Again she met an "Adam" among her early boyfriends, not with a cape, but with a long back wide winter coat, and right through her foreign university, till she met her true soulmate back home in her mid twenties she said that looking back it was like finding her way through a maze of men, or dancing in a masked ball, with glimpses here and there, of the man she was destined to meet. As though her spirit knew the way but teased her.

Most of us, like this young woman, have psychic power, and it try's to guide us, like the inner navigator of our destiny it draws us to possibilities. In becoming aware of this, we can sometimes become more aware of our future. We begin to train our untrained powers..

Spiritual Mentors

Such a person will guide and help you. May teach you to develop your talent or skills. Or to understand yourself and find happiness. The mentor relationship can feel very special like a gift, but usually is one sided, because the mentor spirit, has an edge of higher being or genius in his soul. He has many such people to help or guide in his care. A mentor is someone who gives love and support and understands your talent, in ordinary life he or she can feel like the kind of mother, father, or older sister you always wanted. Teachers, and healers, are often mentors, particular those who specialize, and whom fate seems to have directed your path to cross. Doctors, psychiatrists, Gurus. Psychics, and on the higher non physical level, Angels, Spirits, Guidance from above.

Mentors can some come in the form of historic or dead

people through their teachings, books, or works, if we have a special affinity with their teachings, their guidance will can be more than guidance, and can seem to bring synchronity into our lives. (Synchronity is a series of meaningful coincidences that guide us as if by magic).

Many great people build their works on the basis of someone who has gone before, who was deeply admired. Jung for example was a student of Freud. He developed his works from Freud, and from their split came two schools of thought, where there once had been only one. This is often how new schools of art are formed. How ideas are carried forwards and extended .

A mentor can be in human form, or can be a guide in spirit form, or a historical figure whose works we continue, but most personal mentors have known us in earlier lives in a similar role, and have taken an unconscious vow to help us and lead us again.

A mentor tends to come into life at the time we most need him, like an answer to a silent prayer, when we have wandered on the wayside of life, lost, or at the time when we have a gift or talent to developed and give the world. Such relationship can feel very personal and special, and are of the soul, but unless our soulmate is such a being, they do not always involve romantic involvement or marriage. A mentor of the same sex is particularly important as they act as role models.

Astrological clues; Jupiter aspects are involved in the synastry, also aspects between the ninth house cusp of one persons chart and important significator in the others chart

There may not be very many aspect connections between the charts if the person is only a mentor not a soulmate, because the relationship itself may not be all that enduring or that intimate. It will be for a fixed time or era in life, not forever.

But if love is involved in the relationship, if your Venus or ascendant, conjuncts your soulmates, or lovers ninth house cusp , the soulmate relationship will have something of the Mentor in it. If your Venus contacts his Jupiter, he may be your teacher, or he may be a spiritual mentor.

Soulmate in the Making

Someone special in this life, who unlocks part of your past or future, who heals some wound inside of you, or completes one part of you. A person you may again associate with more closely in future lives. Many close relationships and friendships fall into this category

What to look for in the chart.

Astrological clues; love aspects in synastry, but tending to be connected to the eleventh house or third house and their rulers and signs.

Business

There are business soulmates too. They are usually brought together at a junction in time, that later is recognized as a turning point in both peoples lives. Their karmic purpose is to work together create a business, to invent something together, to devise a system or a theory, or to support or help develop each others unique talents and gifts and help perpetuate them.

To turn an existing idea or business into its next phaze. Each partner can provide what the other lacks in business. When two people get together and invent something original and both profit, so does mankind. The partners may have worked together before in former lives, or they may have each perfected their own skills through past lives separately and be meeting for the first time. But the relationship usually feels fated.

We may have many business partners, but the soul one is the one who brings the right balance. Your other half. A combination of unique talents, the relationship is not always personal, though it can be, both tend to give their dedication to the entity, the business, the invention, or the thing worked on, rather than to each other. Like the parents of a child, the business is more important than their own separate lives and interests. The most notable business soulmate are often in the world of science and invention, the innovators of the past and present..

What to look for in the chart

Astrological clues; the synastry connections are with the midheaven and the tenth house of the charts. The connections may or may not involve romantic aspects. There are usually a lot of aspects and connections between the two charts, even though they may not necessarily be romantic connections. In a natal chart Venus or the seventh house ruler in the tenth can predict a soulmate who will come into your life through your occupation, or his work or through mutual business connections.

Spiritual Family

The definition of a spiritual family, is people we meet in the course of our long life who are not related, but with whom the bond is as close as if they were our own family. Someone who is like a special brother or sister to us, who has a mentality that seems closer to our own, than our own family. Even if they are not like us they understand us, they are there for us when we need them, we are always there for them, we will fight fiercely to defend them, we will shelter them when they need help, we will nurture them when they are ill and there is a cherished bond that may last a life time. Some such people have a parental role, the spiritual mother or father, who sets us an example or helps and guide us in the way our own parents could not. Finding ones spiritual mother can be rather like an adopted person finding their real mother and getting on well with her. It may in no way diminish the bond with their actual mother, it simply enhances their life. There is an affinity, more than that, it compels something. These people have usually been close relatives in a past life, but in the present life are born into different families and scattered across the world, to compete something in their own karma..

What to look for in the chart

Astrological clues; people whose planets fall in your third may be a spiritual sister or brother, tenth and forth houses connect with parents. Moon in third house your sister in this life may have been your mother in the last life or visa versa, Jupiter, same but father, Mars or Venus in third, a lover in the past life may be a sibling in this or visa versa.

Spiritual Home.

A town or country that is not ones home or birth place, but, where you visited once and feel you belong there. A place with a special affinity, it may evoke past life memories or knowledge or strange dreams, like finding a spiritual family, something that was missing before always falls into place after having found your spiritual home. You are happier, no longer a stranger on earth. Usually there is history of feeling you don't quite belong, in your own town, or country but not knowing why. You may feel like an outcast, or you may feel just vaguely out of place. It's because the subconscious memories of the past life place are too powerful, even if they are under the threshold of conscious memory where we cannot know them, they are powerful enough to bond with the past life environment more than with the present. It can also mean a future destiny in such a town or city that is important. For in our lives its not only the past karma we deal with, we build up a future one.

What to look for in the chart

Astrological clues; when the ruler of the fourth house is retrograde, there are subconscious memory's of a spiritual home. The twelfth house ruler, situated in the fourth house can have a similar effect. Neptune in the third or fourth house can have an inborn sense of not belonging in the locality of ones present life birth place. The ninth and tenth and fourth house planets and signs give a clue, planets occupying these houses, make it more likely than empty houses.

Does Everyone Have a Soulmate.

I believe everyone has a soulmate, but some people seem to have immense difficulty in coming together with that destiny. When a soulmate chart is being prepared, what we look for first are testimonies of "marriage." A marriage in this sense is a joining, or being together for a long time. It doesn't necessarily mean a religious or legal wedding. A "testimony" in a chart, is a good planet that shows the likelihood of "marriage". The more testimonies in the chart the more likely the person is to marry.

To find the soulmate. If a person has no fate to marry, there are always certain other signs on their horoscope chart. These signs are called "afflictions". In astrology s antiquated terms an affliction is the opposite of a testimony. For example if a planet with a negative or obstructive influence is aspecting the cusp of house of marriage, say Saturn or Uranus; it is regarded as an affliction. (Unless you're born under Capricorn or Aquarius, for ones own ruling planet is never an afflicter) This affliction will lessen the chance of marriage. But for a person not to marry at all there has to be several afflictions. I have known people with three afflictions and they have still found their soulmate.

The astrologer methodically weighs the testimonies against the afflictions and makes a judgment. This is a lengthy process and it's usually done before ever he begins the reading or writes anything on the page..

If two people's charts are involved, as in synastry, the same assessment has to be done on both charts. Then they both have to be compared to see if one person's planets create an affliction in the other persons chart.. This is why astrology can be expensive, a lot of work and time that the client never knows about goes in behind the scenes. For anyone learning astrology, you must try to be as methodical as this so as to avoid misjudgment. The fewer opportunities left for error to creep in unnoticed, the more accurate your prediction will be.

Most people will find a soulmate eventually. Few people are destined to be alone. But for some the path is far lonelier than for others. Astrology can predict the soulmate in great detail and guide the person towards their best chance of finding love. It can say approximately when they might meet. It an also show if there is some obstacle that needs to be removed from their life first and it can show if there is a diminished chance of meeting a soulmate. Astrology can predict the future husband, lover or partner, who may or may not be a true soulmate. A chart will show if there is no soulmate. I find that unexplained elements seem to draw people who feel impelled to have their soulmate reading done to me at a time in their lives when the soulmate may be not that far ahead as though their inner spirit has brought them to me at the right time to know their future.

If you despair of love and the empty days ahead, I want you to know that it is never as bleak as it feels. Everyone has a future, everyone has a love or some kind or other waiting in that future, if it's not a soulmate, it's a dear friend, or husband of some kind. Don't feel afraid to have a reading, don't feel afraid to learn about astrology or your own chart. Astrology will never destroy you but loneliness might. Loneliness is corrosive, Astrology can take the sting out of being alone, and show you your purpose, your future love.

A Sample Reading

To have your soulmate chart prepared for you is a unique and thrilling experience. It may delight you, it may chill you, it may send a shiver through you of fear, excitement or trepidation, but it will not leave you unmoved.

To illustrate how astrology describes your soulmate. I have chosen two charts from history. Two people with a love story that was both tragic romantic, slightly mysterious. A love affair that made its mark on the modern world. The reason for choosing these particular examples, is simply that History can confirm the charts and the accuracy of astrology can be best demonstrated this way. The charts I have chosen are classical ones. So that even if you don't know a lot about astrology, you will begin to understand the way that astrology is done.

This chart is ill fated in love.

This man has the fixed star Praesepe, the manger in opposition with his marriage house. Praesepe's celestial influence is said to bring disgrace, calamity and eye diseases.

This star was known in ancient china as "The spirits of the ancestors" and is said to give peculiar experience with the realms of the dead. Charles love life was ruled by ancestry, or the spirits of the ancestors in many different ways. His link with Diana also brought the dark fate of her death, Praesepe is quincunx to Saturn. Saturn is the planet of death and history. Saturn, and Uranus are the rulers of his marriage house, they also rule his house of death. It shows his marriage was doomed to end in death. It is also as though Diana's death was doubly fated, both in her own chart and his. An inescapable destiny. A quincunx is a hard aspect I always look on it as being like the seam in a garment, the point where if enough pressure is applied from different directions the person, or their life will be rent apart.. In the years before and after Diana's death, Charles private life, his marriage and reputation were all being destroyed and torn apart in various ways.

So was Diana's life and as this aspect is in the house of soulmates, it's a curse that effects two people not one. An ill fated relationship. But Uranus the ruler of Charles house of marriage was retrograde at his birth. A retrograde planet delays things until much later in life and the bad fate of this marriage, the shadows did not begin to creep out until much later on .In the beginning the love affair and the wedding were a chocolate box romance.

The fifth degree of Aquarius being on Charles house of marriage, describes a tall woman, fifth degree is tall never short, and it is a thin degree. So we have a tall thin woman. The Moon also aspects, it gives a delicate or fair complexion, and this degree, sandy or dark honey color hair. That is how we begin to build up the description in soulmate chart. (The first few degree of Aquarius are ruled by Saturn planet of death, it is Saturn who rules the bones, he has a long, tall, thin, delicate frame. Not raw boned, or skeletal as Saturn usually is, because mercury aspects too, and mercury is boyish, childish. So we have a tall girlish woman, without much flesh or curves. The hair color is worked out in similar way. We know for example her skin is fair with a goods complexion because the Moon aspects the house. The Moon is pale and white, but mingled with the rays of Aquarius, it becomes light pink. The Moon also affects the eyesight. A tendency to look upwards and to the side.

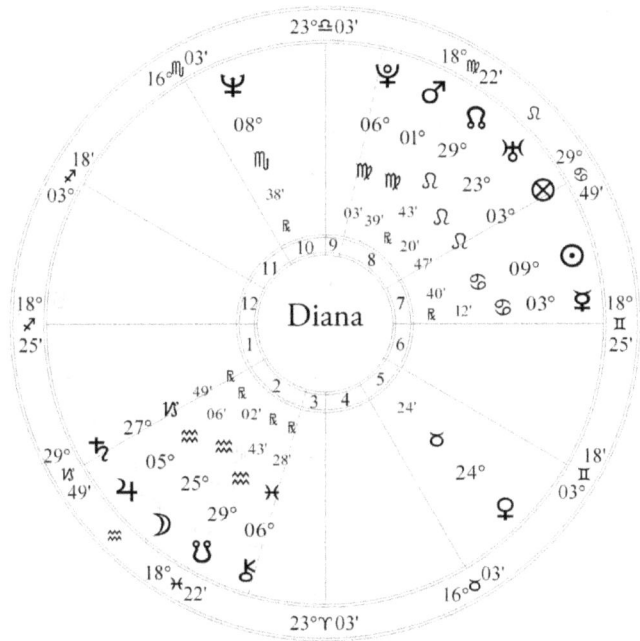

And the eyes close together. The Moon is shyness and so it gives her an almost shy manner of appearance. Aquarius rules the color blue, and lilac, so Charles' bride would be a blond lady with blue eyes.

As we work with the description we can build a more and more detailed picture of Diana, in a soulmate reading for a client I will spend several hours working on the exact description, exact hair shades, and exact shape of the facial features before I go on to other things, like determining the initials. Or the character. But this glimpse into working out a description is enough to illustrate how one persons chart reflects their soulmate or marriage partner.

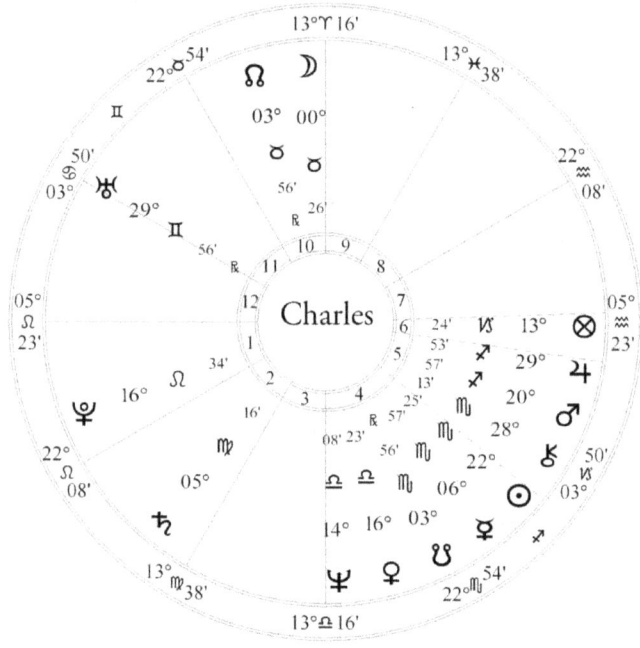

Interestingly the Moon (Moon in tenth means popularity) also aspects Charles marriage house from his own tenth house. The tenth house is the house of one's Career. This aspect points to a famous or popular wife. Diana became more famous than Charles. She will be more dramatized and remembered in history than him. Were they Soul mates? Or is this just a marriage chart?

In Diana's chart her Luna nodes and Moon fall in Charles eighth house, along with her Uranus. The eighth house is the house of death and reincarnation, we can conclude that Diana knew Charles in a past incarnation. So they were soulmates, with a karmic debt to balance, but the debt was paid when Chares married her, enabling her to have her Career. The karmic purpose of the relationship was for Diana's career. If I have lost you dear reader, merge the meaning of the aspect of Charles own Moon, with Diana's planets in his eighth house. You will see why I have arrived at this astrological conclusion. In any chart we read all the aspects together, we read the book, not just the sentence or chapter.

Coming back to spirit of the ancestors. Charles link with Camilla, his second Soulmate, is both karmic and ancestral. Camilla's life and spirit is intricately bound with, or overshadowed by her ancestral grandmother's spirit. Who was also the lover or mistress of an important royal in History. Camilla is almost like a reincarnation or a twin Spirit of this grandmother. Looking at Charles chart (for astrologers, Uranus ruler of 7th is the planet of divorce, Uranus rules sudden breaks and changes, it represents the end of one marriage, it is also ruler of the death house. Illustrating the end of the first marriage in divorce or death or both. Uranus is in Gemini, sign of the twins, showing he would marry or find a Soulmate again. The ruler of Gemini is Mercury, conjunct to the Luna node, it suggests that this second marriage is karmic and ancestral. And it is still shown by unfortunate stars, so the tragedy of Charles love life may not be over yet.

A Woman Called Yoko.

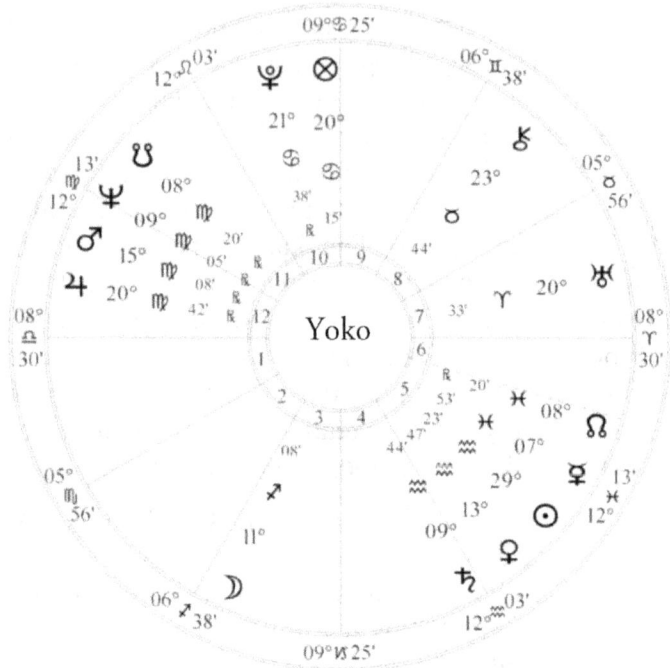

Yoko Ono was born with the Sun in Aquarius, the sign of the arts, her Sun sign is strong in the fifth house. House of creativity. Libra the sign of peace was on her ascendant. And her ruling planet Uranus is in the house of soulmates.

An unusual artistic and talented person with an unusual chart. Uranus in this chart is her ruling planet and so it works more positively than it would in some charts. But it still means a marriage that at times would be unstable. An unconventional marriage to a man of unusual talent who may be either a genius or eccentric, an originator.

Neptune, the planet of overseas places, is conjunct to Mars the ruler of Yoko's marriage house and also makes a quincunx aspect to the cusp of Yoko's house of marriage. This suggests the she was destined to marry a foreigner. The cusp of her house of marriage was Aries (The sign which rules England) Uranus also in Aries. So an English foreigner was always a possibility. Though Aries rules other places too. To really predetermine where her husband came from, we would need to apply other methods. We can go on to describe him from her chart, just as we described Diana from

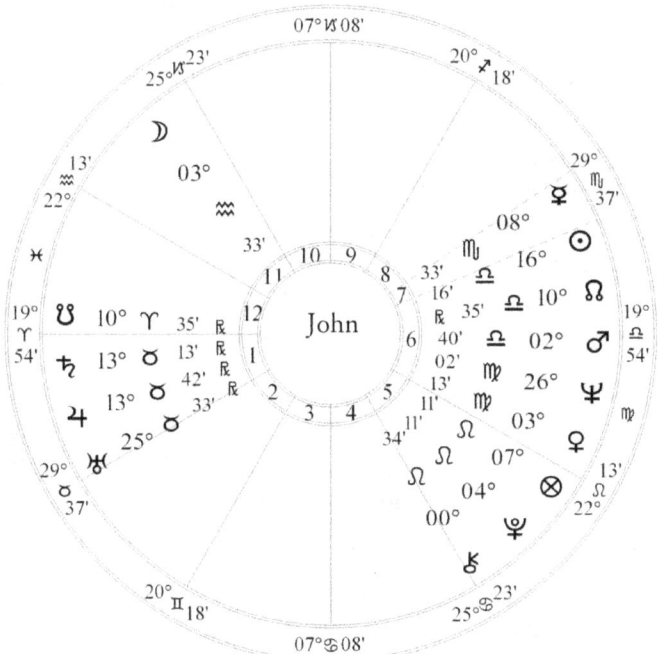

Charles chart. Neptune is conjunct her Luna node, so we even know he might be musical. But let's complete the story instead.

Aries is new beginnings, Uranus, ruler of the arts, in this house, shows that part of this relationship purpose was to do with talent a new creativity, it is likely both Yoko's art, music and creativity and Johns music changed direction for what it would have been. And produced something new, this was their soul's true purpose. Though the ruler of the marriage house being close to Jupiter, they probably thought their mutual souls purpose was to help bring peace to the world.

Mars the marriage house ruler is fractionally into the twelfth house, house of secret enemies. Difficulty's and limitations, the marriage would sometime be troubled, difficult, but this hidden from view, being the twelfth house. And Mars is violence, in this house secret violence, the assassin. Like the other chart there is a hint the marriage would end in death. Venus is conjunct with Yoko's Saturn, a classic symbol of love and death. Though the hint of tragedy in this chart is more complex. They tried to put peace and light in the world, but darkness crashed in on them like the bad side of the balance.

In Yoko's house of marriage coming back to Uranus in Aries, Uranus symbolizes sudden begins and sudden shattering endings. This relationship had both. Neptune is conjunct the Luna node, so this was a fatal karmic attraction that Yoko and John were powerless to resist.

This is real astrology at work. Its mystery and its logic, which are always combined for you in my readings.

The pattern that is reflected in your Natal chart, is as unique as your fingerprint, and as unique as the love you will find. No one has this same cosmological pattern.

The soulmate is unique to you. What else does the soulmate chart tell you? It will reveal his character, his initials, his age, background, it will give an insight into the fate of the marriage and the karma.

Synastry

Synastry, also called chart Comparison or Compatibility is a technique where your astrology chart is compared to the chart of someone you love. The two charts are like two separate pieces of a jig saw when you put them together a picture emerges that could not be seen before. This picture is a portrait of the relationship between you. It may show if you are soulmates,

There are many ways that a soulmate connection can show between two astrology charts. When an astrologer examines the chart the whole chart and every aspect and angle is taken into account, not just a few factors. Synastry readings also give an insight into what the future is, and how you relate to each other. It is a very complex form of astrological analysis, and it is used in relationship counseling as well as predicting. In modern times fewer astrologers predict, it is becoming a lost art.

To be able to predict the future, which you will learn to do from my books, doesn't means all things are fixed unchangeably in fate, it only means we can look down a road into the distance, we can glance at what is there, for however detailed astrology sounds, it is only a glimpse seen through a window, and then having done so, we can then pick our way down the path, making our own decisions and own way carefully. Destiny is not the reverse of free will, rather they work in tandem. To know destiny means you are nobody's puppet, not even the gods.

Synastry aspects between charts.

Mars and Venus aspects of any kind, especially conjunctions, oppositions and squares. These usually mean a sexual attraction. The potential to be lovers, but by itself it does not indicate a soulmate bond, there needs to be many more connections. But if it is there along with other things it certainly adds to the likelihood.

Luna Nodes, connections between one persons Luna node and planets, house cusps in the others chart. This means a relationship that is karmic and so it will feel more powerful than an ordinary relationship. You may have met before, in the avenues of time, other lives, other places, you have old karmic situations to revisit, unfinished matters. It does not necessarily mean the relationship is also a Soulmate one, but very often it is a strong indication that it is. This is more so if the Luna nodes of both charts make some kind of aspect to each others chart. The exact details and nature of such a relationship and often its future outcome can be decided by the aspects itself.

Eighth house reconnections, aspects to the eighth house cusp, planet in the other person eighth house, the eighth house is death and reincarnation, it can be an indicator of soulmate relationship,

Ascendant - Descended Conjunctions.

When your ascendant conjuncts his descendant or visa versa, it means he is your altar ego, and you are his, the mirror of each others soul ; it is a common aspect in the attraction of opposites. Depending on what else is in the charts, it is a compelling aspect, but can mean a complicated relationship. You each have something teach to the other, about the balance between love and self. Or mine and yours. Sharing and selfishness, love and hate.

But remember that we can do a synastry reading from any two charts. Yours and a total stranger, and it would show something. Who knows what!. Perhaps a future that would happen if the two lives become merged into one. But it doesn't automatically mean they *will* merge. This is why if someone wants to know, if this man is a soulmate, I like them to have their Soulmate Charts completed before they consider a synastry, to see if it describes him.

In constructing the synastry we assume there is some existing connection, and a practical realistic link between you. That you know the person. That they area close friend or partner, a past or present lover. If you soulmate chart describe the man, then it is more certain. But it is always very difficult to say for certain if two people will marry from examining their charts. It is only really the strong possibility of marriage that we can determine. Because even if every marriage aspect known to astrology is visible, and it appears in cross aspects between the charts linking them, there are millions of people in the world who's charts may also have similar aspects and links to yours, should you happen to meet up. Keeping this in mind, and knowing the way astrology works can help avert self induced disappointment.

Loved and lost.

What if you have met your soulmate and parted, or he has died? This is not the end, that's the first thing to know, nothing ever really ends. Love continues when the lover is gone, it just changes its face. The past is full of ghosts of former loves and other lives, ancient memory. Where we walk we have walked before. And will again, in this life time or another future, and even if the paths grow cold and apart for a time, this too is destiny and the soul can wait.

The widow weeps but her tears are dried, all suffering ends, but sometimes the path we must walk is dark in patches. Suffering is not to be avoided, but to be walked through, for even the pain is destiny which we learn from. And even the ice desert where we feel nothings. Empty, beyond all pain and not alive, is meant, we walk it and we return form it to the summer. To do so is to keep the faith in love. To try and cut the thorny path short is wrong means we reincarnate next time with the unprocessed pain of this life to add to whatever burden our next life and love carries with, it makes karma harder not easier. When we travel in such dark times, knowing and believing, isn't enough, for a time we loss all faith of belief, that better days will come. But like a shaft of sunlight through darkness the days will be warmed again by love in some form. We will not be alone like this for ever.

When your soulmate dies a part of you dies with him emotionally, like all lost things in life that will not return, but another part lives on, and this is a hard path you must walk but the part that lives on is drawn irresistibly by time towards a future you cannot see. But in that future there is love waiting. The love you have left behind is an unfinished book, you'll comeback to the same chapter in other lives but now you must walk on, the magnitude of your suffering will reflect the magnitude of your love. But nothing lasts forever not even suffering, all things change, they are part of the experience of deep love. In some peoples lives there are many partings many reunions, e.g. retrograde planets in a synastry, Uranus retrograde.

Every life has its winters and its summers. If you are a person who has only one soulmate in a life time. There will be another love, to keep you company, who is perhaps as wonderful, and extraordinary, but not the same, wonderful in a different way. The chart can reveal this too. Emptiness is not allowed to exist in life for long. Eternity can seem to short when you are with a great love. But in one life there are many eternity's many destinies.

Reading the Houses in the Soulmate Chart

The sky is divided into twelve sections in astrology, these are the celestial houses. The cusp of the house is the door , the point where planets enter, the degree and sign that sit on the door step or cusp have an influence over that house. The houses in the soulmate chart have the same meaning as the houses in any chart but with one or two differences.

FIRST HOUSE, This house represents your self, and your personal affairs. The beginning of your life. It is how your soulmate will see you. This house is the image he will have of you from the meeting. It also represents the present incarnation and the Aura.

If you have Mercury retrograde in the first house of your chart, your soulmate may see you as a person who doesn't speak very well, is silent or who doesn't communicate much. Mercury is the planet of communication, in the first house he is speech. Retrogrades obstruct or hold back. If you have Aries in the first house your partner may view you as confident vibrant, outgoing, regardless of whether you are those things. With Scorpio here he may think you mysterious, secretive, and reserved. If you have Virgo here he may think you are always neat and well dressed.

To interpret a house properly you must merge the information given by the house, sign and any planet in it. So if you have Mercury retrograde in Scorpio in the first house you will seem mysterious, you will speak little. You would have secrets and your personal affairs would not be straight forward.

SECOND HOUSE. Your self worth. Your material wealth or poverty. How you will come to influence your soulmates financial affairs and attitudes. What you will gain or come own financially and spiritually with your soulmates help. The wedding breakfast, or wedding feast.

THIRD HOUSE. Your neighborhood. Blood relatives. Karma. Any letters or emails you write your soulmate.

FOURTH HOUSE. Your infancy, your mother;. Your early home with your parents and subsequent homes. Conditions at the end of your life. Real Estate and domestic affairs. All of them influence the relationship.

FIFTH HOUSE, The children of the relationship. Gifts of love. The wedding or engagement jewelry and ring.

Prodigies. Sex life and your bedroom. Your soulmates youth or adolescence is shown in your fifth house.

SIXTH HOUSE, Health and sickness. Working life. The wedding gown; the partner's life before you met. The term of engagement before marriage. Your pets, though some astrologers count the fifth house as pets.

SEVENTH HOUSE. Marriage. The Anima/ Animus; The beginning of the relationship and early years of your marriage. Other partnerships such as business and any binding contracts struck between you and others. Your "astral" or metaphysical bodies.

EIGHTH HOUSE, Death and reincarnation, Ancestry, Genetic and financial inheritance. The Dowry. The partner's money. Taxation, insurance, joint finances, Partners influence on your wealth or poverty. The intermediate years after marriage..

NINTH HOUSE. The " in laws", (Soulmates blood relatives) Strangers. Foreign affairs. Ceremonies that legalize things. The Wedding ceremony or celebration. Faith (whether political or religious) Travel. Psychic matters and all journeys physically or metaphysically into the unknown. Including Dreams and nightmare. Your intellect and your education or lack of it. Angels and Guides.

TENTH HOUSE. The culmination or result; how the relationship will finally work out for you both. Your Career. Your ambitions or achievements. The Father. Other authority figures including the Gods.

ELEVENTH HOUSE. Hope. Friendships; Any clubs, societies or organizations that you may belong to..

Unfaithfulness. The soulmates previous relationships and their legacy on his character and life; Step children.

TWELFTH HOUSE. The past incarnation.. The house of self undoing and secret tasks. The karma carried by the soulmate. Sorrows. Miseries Limitations of any kind, including prisons and institution, serious bad health.. Phobias, madness. Bereavement. The subconscious mind. The hidden elements of love and life. Secrets you keep.

These are the main significations of the houses in a soulmate reading. They are very useful to know. A treasure trove of information is kept in each house. If you a want to know if your soulmate will have money or if he will make a will in your favour, and you do not have his chart, or have not yet met your soulmate, you look to your own eighth house, and to the way it or its ruling planets may configure with your seventh house. The seventh house is the house of soulmates, and any connections between that house or its rulers and the eighth house, by aspect, transit, ruler, or any way at all, will tell you something about the financial relationship. These are all little stitches in the cloth of fate, for us to unravel, in some charts they will provide only minute threads of information, in others something significant will fall out as we pick away at the chart. Even if there are no planets the sign will tell you vaguely how it will be, for some signs are reminiscent of poverty some of wealth. If you want to know about your wedding ceremony, you us the ninth house and its connections to the seventh in exactly the same way.

Psychic Powers and Soulmate Bonds

Some people strongly feel they are near the soulmate in his absence, it goes away, it returns? I think at these times what happens is not always a desire to be near him, or her, it can be the actual spiritual feeling of nearness, an awareness of the close proximity of his spirit, Because at these times. His spirit and yours are in contact on another soul level. This level may be telepathic, or it may be a subconscious psychic awareness of what he is doing, where he is. We all have psychic powers that we are usually unaware of. But because this is hard for the conscious mind to comprehend or interpret on a conscious level, as the conscious only experience a limited amount, (in the same way that we can only remember a fragment of say our dreams which are another level of conscious, even though we think we have recalled it all). So when we experience contact with another soul on a spiritual level, the conscious mind has barriers and you mistake it for desire, as you look for something known to translate this unknown sensation into and makes sense of it. It is only by hindsight that we usually know if such an experience is genuine or wishful thinking.

People who are not usually psychic can become so in connection with various things, one is the soulmate, another is survival. We read of people who have a dream not to buy a ticket for the boat or train, and it crashes. Sometimes we think of a person from years past, and then we cross her path in the street or she writes to us. The spirit has a vested interest in its soulmate, and so it has more incentive to be psychic. Does the soulmate experience this too? The answer is variable. When this happens your soul and his touch in a way that is both powerful and insubstantial. A sensation that is not a sensation, you are drawn to each other, an allurement or compulsion that cannot be defined but is felt. But how much the other person's conscious mind is aware of this depends on their own psychic ability. He may feel the same, may feel more, or less, it depends on how much his conscious is in tune with you or in tune with its psychic powers, some people shut off their psychic powers totally and are aware of nothing, others seem to know much already, I have had a client say to me, that everything I told her, seems to conform what she knew on some level. Each person is at different stages in their psychic development, soulmates have spent a life time not together waiting to meet or perhaps many lifetimes, but they are not necessarily at the same stage.

Reading the Planets in a Soulmate Chart

Like the celestial houses, the planet have a similar interpretive meaning in the soulmate reading to that of any chart, it is just that we focus them more on the relationship.

SUN, Your own Life. Your self. In a woman's chart what she expects or hopes for in a man. This planet being the subconscious influence of her father on her character. The father is the first man to have power over you, the first to make an imprint on your consciousness in the formative infantile years of life, and therefore he is etched on your subconscious ever after like an archetype. This will pre determine what you expect, what you hope and fear and seek in a man, or what you avoid and turn away from. The experience of your father may be blissful or terrible, but it's what you were brought up to be familiar with. Your spirit recognizes it in others. It's what is known, and the known is always more secure than the unknown. It what you allow or welcome. When interpreting the Sun for a soulmate reading, more importance is placed on the aspects its makes, and its relation to other planets and the house that it is.

For example if the Sun is in the first house, she will hope for someone like herself. The father allowed her to be herself, the mother may not have done. If in the second she will hope for a man of money. The father supports the child. The mother may not have done. The Sun is essentially what the father gives you, not what both parents give. The Sun is half of you ,the Moon the other.

A third house Sun seeks someone companionable avuncular or brotherly, someone neighborly. The planets complicate the suns influence. If Jupiter is rising you may consciously seek a man who has all the wonderful quality of your father. Jupiter is the benign, generous, loving father. But suppose the Sun is conjunct to Pluto or Saturn in the first house., the father may have been distant, frightening, oppressive, or some infantile trauma is associated with him. The subconscious imprint or subliminal message is that men you love are frightening, domineering, oppressive, the character may then build up walls of protection, find it harder to relate, or she may seek a man who builds up walls and stays distant, since the Sun is also the self, it seeks the fathers imprint, but it also seeks the sameness of itself, its zodiac sign. With a Saturn afflicted Sun there may always be a barrier between herself and the man, a mistrust of love or fear of love. She may either marry a man who turns out to be frightening and oppressive like the father, even if he seemed like herself to begin with, because it's what feels familiar, and so it's what her inner self guides her towards. Or she may consciously recognize his influence and seek the opposite in love. Or she resists marriage, Saturn is slow to find love, Pluto must overcome trauma before it can love, so she may resists until she finds someone who doesn't frighten or traumatize her.

MOON, Emotions; Maturity of Immaturity. Yourself as a child. In a man's chart what he subconsciously expects or hopes from a woman. This being the subconscious influence of the mother.

MERCURY, Your ability to talk to your soulmate. Letters, emails communications in the relationship. Writing,. Also what you subconscious expects of your children.

VENUS, in a man's chart the kind of woman he seeks. Her love making or her intimate sexual habits abilities. In all charts Venus is love and what we love. Possessiveness and ownership

MARS, in a woman's chart the kind of man she desires. Her soulmates sexual habits and performance. Mars is sexual passion. Also aggression , things you may quarrel about. Rivalry and jealousy.

Mars in the air signs, you desire a man who has intellectual strengths, someone intelligent, or creative. The thinking man. In the earth signs, you want someone to impress you with his physical strength, his money, his material life, his good looks, his job. Mars in the water signs, and you are influenced or attracted by his emotional side. Mars in fire signs and it is his vitality, his ambition, his generosity, showiness, his outgoing qualities

JUPITER, Tolerance; Gain and Reward. What the marriage or soulmate relationship will compensate you, or reward you with. What you will need to be tolerant of. Jupiter is education, so he is also what you will learn in the relationship.

SATURN, Limitation. Loneliness within the marriage., Thrifty. Self denying, cold, what you will be kept short of or denied; Death, Endings Traditions. What you may weep about in love.

CHIRON, The way in which you are different from others. Including disabilities or deformities, irregularity. The area of life where you are most wounded emotionally. Or the thing that is missing in your life. What your soulmate has to heal in you, to make you whole.

URANUS, Originality. Science, invention.. The unexpected way the soul mate relationship will change your lifestyle and new things he will bring into your life. The joining of differences. The alchemy of the marriage.. Non arranged or unconventional relationships.

NEPTUNE, lingering, weakening, Psychic and spiritual things. Liquids glass, transparent, insubstantial things. Distant things. Anything that is mysterious or partly obscured. Deceptions, delusion, addictions. Things about the relationship which are not as they seem to be. The things your soulmate will conceal from you, or you from him.

PLUTO, The dark side of the relationship, or of yourself. The things love will transform. The things that will be kept hidden from others about the relationship.. Destruction and rebuilding. Research, buried things, power Oils. Obsessions. Enemies and opponent. Outside influences, such as the nation, the times we live in and so on, their effect on love..

SOUTH NODE. The past life's karma, and what we are moving away from in our karma.

NORTH NODE. Karma carried forwards from the past life into the present, and what we are taking into the future from the present life

But note that in some charts the nodes seem to work in the opposite way. Both nodes in synastry have to do with soulmate connections.

When A Soulmate Is Not A Soulmate.

A Guiding Spirit in Disguise

One client said to me "Sometimes I feel as though there is no progress and that I am just living in a fantasy that I cannot let go of ". This client was in love with a man who barely recognized her existence. She in turn knew little about him, a figure at a distance, but she imagined much. Her thoughts dwelt on him. No real relationship of any substance existed. He had appeared in a play, but it was as much the role he played that had enchanted her, as the man. For a year she had been unable to stop herself thinking about him. It had slithered from idle moments of reverie to a dark corner of obsession. In her head was a house with a grey stone lion at the door, she wore Italian clothes and held his hand on tower bridge. They drank at wine bar that did not exist. They danced on the moonlit deck of a ship in evening dress. They visited Venice, Milan, New York. All in her head, none of it was real. Only those who have experienced it know the torment of such madness. How can this mystery be explained. Astrologically the two charts showed hardly any synastry connections at all. No cross aspects or connection existed between the charts, just as in real life no connections existed between the two people.

Occasionally people are very lonely, and so desperate for love in their live that they don't simply slide towards illusion, they get locked in an imaginary world of their own making, which becomes akin to a mild mental illness, a madness. If your love is a total fantasy, that has no shred of reality at all, say a character from a film you have never met, or had any contact with and never have a hope of ever meeting, it may be an escape from life, or it may be a distorted kind of spiritual guidance.

Sometimes people are haunted by others for a different reason. Jung, the analyst, was haunted by ghosts all his life. He referred to it as an "assault from the unconscious" he neither wanted it, nor could he get rid of it. A life long battle (but for Jung it had a purpose). He'd first become obsessed with a figure from his imagination. This figure was not a romantic attachment. But it would be with him constantly, so real that he'd have internal conversations with it, and get answers. He'd know its character, its life history. This figure a man he'd called Philemon, was with Jung a number of years and as real to him as living man, and he resented the way this figure filled up his head and got in the way of his life.

Jung met an elderly Indian. This Indian began speaking of his own " spirit guide" as though it were the most natural thing in the world to be accompanied by a mythical or fantasy figure. Previous to this Jung had assumed that he himself was mad ! And he'd spent many years trying to understand and cure his own madness, out of which came some of greatest research work and his greatest theories in the world Philemon, his "fantasy figure" who just wouldn't leave, had a purpose. That was his purpose, to push Jung into becoming a great analyst. Jung then decided that Philemon must be his spirit guide and maybe he was, so his research and struggle with Philemon turned away slightly from psychiatry to mysticism and again this had purpose, a though it was part of Jung's fate to experience this, and extract something from the experience for his work.

Jung felt that figures of romantic fantasy, whether purely imaginary or an actual person were always like a projection of what we needed. The subconscious attempt to heal our life or put something good there. Jung was actually haunted by various fantasies all his life, but not happily. He couldn't enjoy the romantic dream like the rest of us, when we slip into another life and leave the world behind and have tea in the garden with our favorite character, he used to refer to it assaults from the unconscious and when it is difficult and tormenting and wont let you live your life, it feels like that. Like a madness that won't leave.. It was his own discontent with fantasy and his own mind that caused him investigate it and add a new dimension to Freud's work. His own characters were so intrusive they were obsessive, and so took over,

So if it is a fantasy love, its purpose will only emerge in its own time, but it will be leading you towards something. Your task is to try and find what.

An English writer from the 1800s I recall whose characters were as real to him as if they were living beings, so much so that he and his wife used to include them in the conversation. They were often based on people he saw around him like a seed that took on its own form and grew after that. But once the book was written the characters would disappear, and he'd long for the next ones so he could get on with his work. He could write nothing without them. Unlike Jung he enjoyed it immensely, it was an extra dimension to life. But if he hadn't been able to write and profit, he too may have felt that he simply lived in poisoned a fantasy that had no purpose.

Love has many roads, some are the roads of misdirection. But love real or imagined always has a karmic purpose. It can be a challenge to find what it is. Remember everything you do to help eliminate an illusion of love from your life, leads you closer to the fate of the true one. Love is a sacred journey that you make spiritually as well as externally. Some people are fortunate, they meet, they fall in love and there are no complications. But for others , they must walk down many treacherous places; avenues of love and loneliness before they find the right door..

When love becomes a mental illness, the first step to cure it, is the same as alcoholism that is to acknowledge it is a sickness of the soul, not a situation with real possibilities. There is no illusion except what you make yourself. If you do not set aside the curtain of illusion and let reality into your life. Then the future, if any, reflected in the chart, may also contain degree of distortion.. The astrology chart reflects your world. It is only ready to disclose its secrets when your soul is ready. A person can mislead themselves and perhaps in the process mislead the astrologer too. Usually it won't. An astrologer will try to ensure at all time that information he or gives is correct, so that false hope is not given., but the charts of the deeply mentally disturbed, the people who genuinely live in a "different" world, remote from reality are complex. What if you are haunted by a non-existent person? Is there a remedy for it. Yes you "met" your imaginary soulmate in the imaginary worlds, so you can meet the real one in the real world, it is a little harder that's all. When you recognize illness and seek its cure. How?

In astrology there are three steps. When I hear a client say "her love is an impossible hope" I do the same as when I get a client who said he has been diagnosed as persecution complex..

The first step is to look at his chart to see if he is really being victimized. Some people get told they are suffering from persecution complex, when the truth is they are being persecuted!. Just as some people are told their health is psychosomatic and to pull themselves together next day they drop dead! So it is important astrologically to check whether it is a lost cause, this hopeless love, or if in fact they will marry their love, however impossible.

Step two, if it is an impossibility, and nothing can come of such a longing. Then we must determine if its illness, or if a distorted kind of spiritual guidance.

Step three, if its spirit guidance, we have to try and find what the person is supposed to do to set herself free of this possession. Like a jumper that has been put on inside out, it corrects itself. You must try and find what this inner figures purpose is, what he is trying to make you do, or find. Where he is leading you. There will be a purpose that may be something just as transforming and essential to happiness and success in its own way as the soulmate itself. If it is illness, we have to find the psychological cause, and help find the cure.

Delusion or Spirit Guide

Jung thought that the kind of character the person became attached to showed the area of life they needed to mend or work on within themselves. That such a character or person, was always a reflection of an inner messenger or guiding figure guiding us towards something. Like an outer reflection of an inner spirit figure, or an inner fantasy that has manifested for whatever reason in the guise of a real person. Like if someone becomes attached to a power figure, say a leader, it may be because they have been made to feel insignificant in their life, they want to feel important. So the key to mending the psychological wound, is for them to aim at importance, power. If the figure is a hero type rather than a ruler, then the person may have the wish to be rescued from the circumstance in life, in which case again they need to apply themselves to their own rescue and finding their own strength.

I think different men can represent the same thing. The past is important here, if you look at the history of different men, or different obsessions in your life, you might find one common element, and this might give you a clue. If you ask yourself how did they make you feel? Did they make you feel important? Or did they make you feel powerful? Or looked after?. Or pretty? Because whatever one main thing these men you have been drawn to made you feel, the root cause might be someone or something in your life just before that that made you feel the exact opposite, and the man might be a kind of escape fantasy preventing you dealing with that mentally. . When you start getting back to that, thought it might take a few months to make all the realizations, you might find that dreams of this man, or other men who are not available fade away. When it is done the real soulmate appears.

Paths of Misdirection

Finding you way back from paths of misdirection is the only way to find the soulmate. Fate is very powerful, but illusion can block the path. A soulmate is not illusion from the unconscious, other relationships are, Infatuation, sex addiction, unreciprocated loves, attachments to loves ended in the distant past, they are all paths that misdirect the mind into an unhappy labyrinth.

I am reminded of an ancient Babylonian myth about a goddess called Innana, who descended into hell, (the unconscious) in her search for her soulmate, and as she descended level after level , lower and lower, she lost something, her necklace, her dress, her hope, her reason, until she was naked. I am also reminded here of the ancient dance of seven veils, where a lady shrouded in silky gossamer veils dances, a ghost dance, and one by one she sheds her illusions, veil by veil, until her true form is reveled, this is rather like the Innana's symbolic journey to the soulmate. There may be more than seven paths of misdirection or illusion for some of us. But we grasp at various illusions and they cut us like brambles in the wayside, but once we weed them out, or shed them all one by one, the infatuation, the jealousy's, the anima projection, the illusions of love, the ego, the greed, the sexual illusion, the escape from life, old karmic bonds. Once we are consumed or destroyed by the negative shadow love and survive it, we eventually get to the core of truth, the naked light of love, and are transfigured, then we rise, and take back all we have lost on the way. Instead of taking back illusion we take back truth, Instead of hope we take certainty, from being powerless we take back our own power, we exchange loneliness for love, pain for pleasure. Past for future. Our own dreams become realities which are just as beautiful as the illusions

Back to Karma

People sometimes ask if a relationship is so fated, if we are soulmates, then how can it go so wrong? Why are there so many problems? We tend to assume if it's the right person, it will all go right of its own accord and cant be this pain. But karmic bonds are old and they often have the unfinished karma of many lifetimes wrapped up in them. Problems that were not resolved in the last life are handed down or carried forward into this life, along with the love and pain and intensity of it all like an inheritance. And these things have to be resolved before there is total happiness. Karmic relationships are not always painless but they are always utterly compelling. It is likely that in the past life you experience the same difficulties, but in that life you did not manage to overcome the problem, so it was carried forward in time, it is presented to you once again like a hurdle in this life, different time, place and circumstance, but still the same core problem to resolve, that is the karma or work of the relationship. And that is another reason why you must persevere this time. Otherwise it will all just be carried over into the next life, when you meet him or her again.

This chapter is of greater interest to those who are into Karmic astrology than those who want to predict. But it's worth stating that the future is always built on the past, and so can sometimes be predicted from the past.

Karma of Planets in the Seventh House

Saturn in your seventh house, shows that the soulmate relationship may be based on karmic debts. Karmic issues may be betrayal of love of trust. Mistrust, one person may be a burden on the other in some way, also separations. But this planet is better in some signs than others. It can also indicate the souls mate was linked to you by business partnerships in former lives.

Uranus, in the past life you may have broken away from the soulmate, because one partner advanced spiritually, materially or in terms of character and the other did not. You were two people originally alike, but who as time went on matured and changed into dissimilar characters.. In the present life the soulmate may be someone unusual you did not envisage yourself with. Someone who causes you to have to over come the differences between you. These big differences may be material, like class, colour or race, age. Or more supple difference in creativity and individuality character. Such a relationship will pull you together but radically change both your lives.

Luna nodes in seventh. A soulmate relationship that brings out your karmic purpose in this life. This aspect also suggests a past life that was an arranged marriage of a kind, where you were also married to his family. Depending how well you got on with them in that life., in the present life you will again be tied by circumstance to his family, either embraced in family circle and feeling you have gained not only a husband but a whole wonderful close wider circle of people, or else difficulty with in laws, and power struggles, the feeling of being fettered unwillingly to his family, that he has not grown up and is still governed more by his family than his union to you.

Neptune In the past life you and he may have been separated by distance, seeing each other only rarely. If the gulf between you could not be bridged successfully then in life there is also like to be distance, it may be geographic, emotional, or the distance that one social level of society has to another falling for someone out of reach, or some who has distanced themselves and cannot be reached mentally. In some charts it can represent a soulmate you disappointed or let down badly in a past life and have to make recompense by support or rescue in some way in this life. Or visa versa, one who will rescue you in some way. Much depends on the sign and aspects to Neptune.

Pluto ancient power struggles, secret liaisons. Subconscious memories of danger, catastrophes, holocausts, trauma and fear surround the past life relationship and a curtain of secrecy. The possibility of having been united with your soulmate at a difficult time in history and events of the nation, having some influence or bearing on your past life. Destruction, or devastation of surroundings and a change of direction, empty new beginnings Beware of thinking you have everything under control, because that is when fates steps in to prove to you that there are forces no one can control.

Jupiter lust, greed gluttony and indulgence, older excesses in the past life and powerful material temptations that spoiled the relationship. The present life prosperity or excess, that may raise you upwards, but you have to overcome temptations and avoid excesses this time. There is also something of a teacher student relationship, or mentor and guide and protector relationship wrapped up in the karma. Guidance and inspiration. You must turn from the appetites of the world to the hunger of the mind. Karmic lessons about the value of money and material things. Issues about things that are more important than money or possessing things. If they are positive the lessons learned will feed the mind, if they are negative, they will deplete your worldly wealth..

Chiron, A relationship that was physical or mentally damaging, or the reverse, one that brought healing to your spirit after it was wounded by earlier loves. Medicine. Justice or Law, and the physical body, accidents, sudden crisis, illness and injustice had an influence on the past life union.

Mars a past life relationship to do strong passions and

anger, a love hate relationship, conquest. The soulmate may be an enemy who is now a friend and lover. There may be karma to do with intrigues, passion, violence, war, jealousy or sex. The lesson you have to learn is that love is not a battle ground. To rely on your inner strength and have faith. There will be something you have to conquer in the soulmate relationship. The element Mars occupies can reveal more, earth is something physical or worldly, to be conquers in the course of the relationship, such as illness, addition, violence hardships; Air the conquest is intelectual; water its emotions that you must triumph over, If the relationship is to be happy ,and fire you must fight against, jalousies, cruelties, actions, to win happiness.

Mercury a soulmate relationship with misunderstanding. The past life may have been a child hood or teenage bond, in this life you are reunited to grow up a little more together and allow the relationship to mature,. There may be difficulty in settling down or with commitment. At very best it can represent a twin spirit relationship within the soulmate bond.

Venus the karma around the past life and love will be happy in this life. It was about love, contentment and kindness.

Moon the past life one person may have child parent relationship. Issues of immaturity, family attachment, dependency, moodiness and instability have to be resolved. There may also be karmic challenges about making a new home with the soulmate.

Sun The person may be a twin spirit as well as a soulmate.

Advanced astrology

The ruling planet of your seventh house, and your own ruling planet when in aspect to each other shows what sort of karmic purpose may be unlocked by the soulmate. For example if the ruling planet of your seventh house falls in your first house, house of your private life, the karmic purpose of the relationship will be personal. It may increase your self confidence, or improve your standing, it may change something within you by changing your private life. If Saturn, the planet of limitation, endings, coldness and the past was in your first house it may change your personal life by helping you break away from a restrictive past, or from personal isolations and poverty, or from any of the other things Saturn represents in the first house. We can then add another link to the chain by following the same road through the chart, if Saturn happened to be in Cancer, the limiting background may be the family parents and the home you grew up in., since Cancer presides over those things. Taking next the ruler of *that* house, in our example it's the Moon which rules Cancer. If the ruler of the first house then falls in the tenth. The soulmate will bring changes to your personal life as stated before, then over a period of time he will help or inspire you to build up your life purpose through your Career. He may induce you to change that Career, (Tenth house is career, the sign and any planet will tell us more about that career). We can then continue to work our way around the chart add another page to our story by looking where the tenth house ruler leads us. Eventually we will end up where we began and this chapter of our story is completed. This method is just one way.

Because our book is aimed at all levels, Lets now rest the mind and come back to some simplified astrology and soulmates.

The Signs on the Seventh House

Aries

The soulmate relationship will bring a new phaze in your karma together. Both of you will start out on a new path together, but this path will not be possible before you meet him/her. It is something you cannot do alone, or may not even be aware you want to do before you meet. You are a catalyst in each others lives, united by love everything becomes possible, you are young souls who will find the strength and energy to forge ahead and succeed in a new and hopeful future.

Taurus

Past incarnations have united you and your soulmate together through lives where you and he studied and explored subjects that would have been considered controversial and taboos, the dark areas. Research into the mysteries of life. Psychology, the occult, human sex lives or reproduction, abortion, contraception, perversion. Radical politics. Life's dark extremes. These may still hold a fascination for your soulmate. Karmic issues are about strength of will, transfiguration of your lives, through finding mutual ambitions. Transforming struggle and opposition into Struggling together against adversities, rather than power struggles with each other.

Gemini

The soulmate relationship was happy, healthy, natural, wholesome and rural, and nice in the past life. You are encouraged to come back together in this life, because you have something to teach the world, a wisdom to give out. You have already learned about forgiveness, spirituality or religion and mutual sharing. The giving of love and reciprocation with each other. Healing, tolerance and teaching each other and amassing and cultivating the wealth of the spiritual and material world. You may also have traveled and worked with nature. In this life you have to expend on these concepts to share your understanding, your love, tolerance and mutual wisdom, natural skill and unconditional love with others.

Cancer

The soulmate relationship karma was bare and not very emotional it had to do with business, work, duty, drudgery, practical physical things. In the present life there may be a special karmic task or karmic purpose to complete together. There could also be a past life situation or master and servant type roles, where one partner was kept in luxury, not expected to work, and the other was the drudge, the milk cow, or the one responsible as worker and provider. In the present life there may be burdens, poor health, issue about money or work and equality.

Leo

The soulmate bond is creative artistic, intellectual, experimental or different. In the past life you were ahead of your times and had a relationship that broke away from the old traditions, and bonds and roles allotted by the society you lived in. In some way in the present life this is continued, the relationship will open up startling new paths together. The karmic purpose is to develop your independence your originality, or creativity, and with the help of the soulmate contribute something exciting and controversial and new to the world.

Virgo

You will yearn to meet your soulmate and be together; but with this sign you may in some unaccountable, unpredictable way both end up with other people, or find yourselves living so far apart.

Past life lesson about making scarifies for love, about unrewarded love, unconditional love, the river of tears, and long tests of faith, lingering addictive love, losses, loves strengths and weakness. Past life problems and karma are still being worked through. But when you complete them or find closure, everything moves to a higher happier level, a new cycle begins that embraces the old and continues onwards.

Libra

Building your life round your soulmate.. Part of the karma of this sign is about gender, females may find some aspect of the soulmate relationship puts them in a role or a situation that in the past would belong traditionally to the men of the family. A male role breadwinner or house repairer for example, while males may find they take on a more feminine roles, or child carer, house keeper. A karma that involves a certain degree of role reversal in the relationship. Also issues about duty love fairness and independence. Too much may have been sacrificed by one person in the past life, in this life circumstance will ensure that over time burdens and sacrifices demanded become more shared, more mutual and equal .

Scorpio

You are both old souls who have had many life time together, so the relationship is likely to be stable comfortable and secure, The Love enduring. Through this relationship you will come into your own in life and Providence will work within it. You will support each other, you have much wisdom and intuitive understanding, may be initiated into old mysteries and occult wisdom together, or may each have unique skills, and will build up something enduring or solid to give to the world.

Sagittarius

There are difficult conditions from the past life to do with responsibilities , faithfulness and making a strong single commitment to just one person. You fall in love too fast, you have a secret fear of being imprisoned by love, and tied too restrictively. Your independence curtailed. Love is full of emotional and mental learning for you, your soul is young, restless a wandering spirit and afraid not to be in control in its own life. You have to learn about surrendering to another. Fidelity, reliability, sharing love, and making an enduring relationship will be the challenge. One partner may be unfaithful physically or mentally. You'll be friends , lovers, enemies, so many things rolled into one, so much to learn about love. Lessons are about openness and truth. And endurance.

Capricorn

The soulmate relationship will feel familiar and right to you, like family. In the past life you were part of the same tribe, community, or extended family, part of the same and soul groups. In the present life the lessons of the relationship are about maturity and immaturity, cycles of life, birth, growth, old age, death.

The human life cycle and learning to have courage to turn away from familiar things and places and to strike out of a less traditional path with your soulmate. Soulmate karmic issues may be about family, children, house or home.

Aquarius

In former lives with the soulmate there was a lot of glamour. Tradition, extravagance wealth, and pride. The soulmate will restore this to your life. He will bring you admiration and respect, but the lessons fate will force you to learn will be about spiritual strength, about the individual worth of true love regardless of whether it has success, or wealth attending it, that outer trappings don't matter in the end..

Pisces.

Beliefs, devotion faith, morality and the practical side of life and spiritually were important in the past life. Sexuality and physical health may also have been an important past life element and could have karmic reverberations in this life. Your souls are joined across many lives, where healing, medicine, hygiene, diet, health, pollution, the correspondence between body, mind and soul were important. Working together with your soulmate, helping each other, being useful rather than being used, are karmic issues brought over from past lives. Healing past life damage in the soulmate relationship, so that it embody the purity and perfection you always sought in each other, will bond you together so can then find a way to help to heal the damage and the karma of the world

Karmic Cloths

Karma from relationships can emerge life after life, or relationship after relationship. This karma can be from knowing him personally in a past life and unsolved problems from then. Or it can be more general, the kind psychological of Karma that we carry forward from this life. An example of Karma (which basically means cause and effect) being carried over from relationship to relationship in the present life would be if a woman had a history of badly broken relationships that ended for the same reason.

Let's say her man had secret liaisons, was unfaithful, wouldn't tell her anything, lead a double life. She might then marry a good faithful man, but because she has been so hurt by unfaithfulness in the past, she may never quite trust this man. She may subconsciously be on guard, like a dog at the door, waiting for the day when the past will repeat, to wreck destruction across her life. This will affect the way she thinks, and the way she treats him, it may cause unnecessary jealousy that will be detrimental. It will heighten her mistrust, like an underlying poison in the relationship, the sap of which is always there ready to ooze out. Some times it will come out; it may lead to her making unjust accusations, if he's late home from work, she may suspect he has lingered somewhere with someone attractive, If she restrains herself and doesn't accuse him, she will still store it in her mind. It may cause her to be harsher, to be shorter tempered, to snap more, to pry into his life more. This in turn may make him secretive, in order to retain his privacy. The more secretive he is, the more she pry's, like a spiral of destruction. The more snappish and stinging she is, the more he may retaliate, or avoid her, or spend less time at home. If she exhibits jealousy conjured from some threat when he speaks to his friend's wife, he will make sure she doesn't find out next time he speaks to a friend's wife. The most mistrustful she is, the less valued and more misjudged he feels. Things escalate; relationship weaken when people stop relating. And soon no relationship exists. He does find someone else, what she fears become reality. It confirms her original judgment, that all men are unfaithful. These self perpetuating things will carve the shape of her future, like another ring of bark round a tree , each one fore dooms the next relationship. This is karma repeating.

If she could clearly see the "karma" and understand her own part in its perpetuation, it need not repeat. If she reinforces the positive knowledge that this man is not her previous man, he is a different character, that history need not repeat, then she can work to understand change her own negative fears and their spiraling effects on her behavior and the wider effect on relationship. Then the relationship will strength not weaken. In short the psychological karma makes or breaks the relationship, and is acted out in various ways. This is true of past life karma too, but past life karma can be more mysterious and complex. The main thing is to be able to recognize and identify the problem and work on it, so the relationship and your understanding is strengthened, rather than diluted by imagined fears that have not yet materialized. Because of the nature of karma it is not always possible predict in advance specific events or difficulties related to it.

Past life Karma is not all punishing or hard work, as our next example will reveal, but holds a hidden key to the foundations on which the present life is built.

Example of Karmic Synastry Question.

Question

Claire's question was that she had met a man and she could not get him out of her thoughts. This had never happened before to her. Why had he such a haunting effect? Was there a possible relationship or future with him?

The man, Frank, had gone to work in Belgium taking the post of history teacher in a private school, and out of her life, but he maintained a friendship with Claire by letter

Answer For Claire

I have drawn up both charts. On your own Natal chart the very interesting thing is that you have a Venus, conjunct with Pluto both in the second degree of Virgo, in the house of love and marriage. Pluto has to do with the subconscious, and also with Karma and obsession. (Venus is the planet of love, and this aspect reveals subconscious memories of an old karma before birth; past life memories, that have re awoken or stirred in their sleep by the meeting, but not enough to surface to conscious perception)

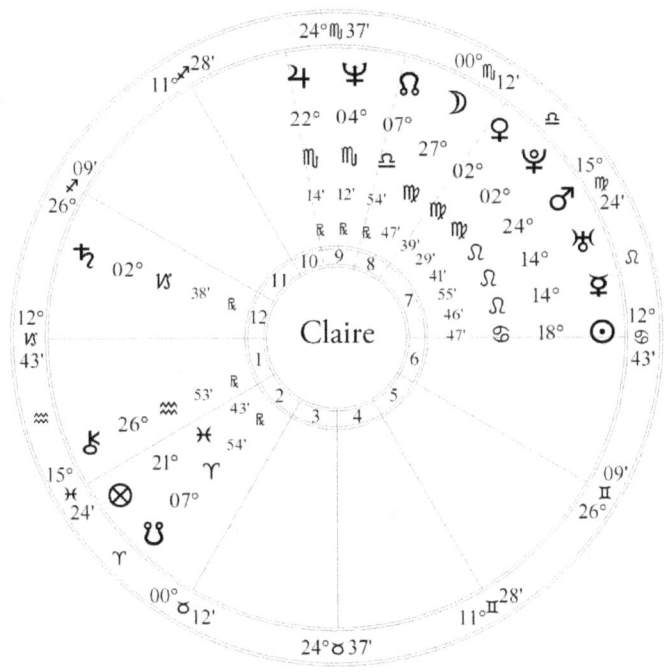

Neptune in your ninth house also aspects and conjuncts his Neptune in his twelfth house (his house of subconscious memories). This casts a veil, a romantic gossamer mist over things, this veil is felt not seen, like a dream that seeps into the soul. Venus is love. Now this Neptune aspect is retrograde, or dormant, "switched off" in the natal chart at birth. So you go about your normal life for years and this dreamy deep kind of magical romance never intrudes. No matter how much you would like, life retains its coldness, and love its remoteness. But when this aspect is " switched back on", or woken by a transit, or in this case by the man's chart aspects inter reacting with yours, it has the power to move your life, to change everything that has been dormant within you. This is what has happened.

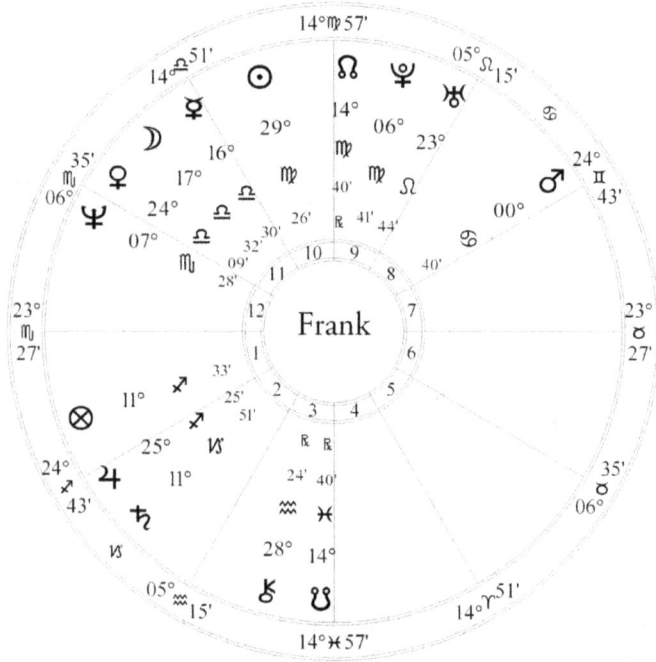

At the very best such an aspect has the power to bring a soulmate, at the very least to make something unusual, enchanting and romantic fall like a cloth of dreams over your eyes and life. Such episodes are rare in life so we must enjoy them, even the pain and mystery of them. That is my first advice. Life's tapestry is made richer by such things. The way the aspect brings a romantic encounter of this type, is because your subconscious (Pluto) knows that you have known your true soulmate in a past life and it is waiting for him to return, so it responds to other past life or karmic connections. Or ones that remind the subconscious of him, like a false recognition, or a real recognition..

His Luna node (Karma) conjuncts your eighth house cusp (house of death and reincarnation) showing a past life link between you. The Neptune aspects in the synastry also tells us that you have met before. The past life took place in a different country. Neptune is foreign lands, and Pluto unknown places (Though the charts suggest Holland, rather than Belgium. Readers may wonder how I came to that conclusion!

Why Holland? I came to it astrologically, as I do with all the statements made in this book. It is an advanced form of astrology which I will cover in one of my other books, for now lets keep to Claire's question) So subconsciously Claire, you have recognized this man as a soulmate, regardless of whether he is or not. That is why he haunts you. That's the answer to the first part of your question. This man may , or may not be not be your soulmate, it depends if your soulmate chart describe him.

His Saturn conjuncts your ascendant. This often brings a meeting and parting, as it has done in this life sometimes followed by a depression. As Saturn rules parting, a rise of emotion and a fall of them. But there is hope for a future meeting and future involvement because there are some cross aspects between and retrograde aspects between your charts. You have your Moon in Virgo ,the same sign and degree as his Sun. This connects your two charts directly. This is a classic friendship aspect, it also shows there is no dream here, no misguidance, only reality. Though it needs other aspects to strengthen it before anything solid can come of the relationship. The strongest pull is that you have met him in a past life in a different country. His Saturn square his Neptune, rules cold and enduring rain. You met (your ascendant is the meeting) on a rainy night, when it had rained for days. At a gathering to do with inheritance and money. In an old family house, with a lot of dark brown painted wood floors and staircase and two tone painted walls of green on the top and brown on the bottom. Stair rail of carved wood (Again my dear reader you will be wondering how this description was obtained, but just as person can be described from a chart, so can a room, or a place, or a building. It is not really so difficult.) Saturn is a grim and serious planet, and linked to the ascendant, the ascendant is the beginning of the chart and so symbolizes the meeting, the meeting was under gloomy circumstance. Astrologically in the synastry his Saturn suggests the meeting was linked to a death. His connection with the family was through legal work. Your connection in that life was family, some kind of relative and an inheritance.

Franks tenth house cusp, house of work, is conjunct her eighth house, house of death - symbolizing his work regarding a death. The eighth house has to do with the past life, ancestry and inheritance. Her Sun in Cancer (family, home) opposite his Saturn - a death in her family. The house and setting can be described in the same way a person can, as previously illustrated. Planets have their colors and their substances, their shapes and form. I have cut this extract short, it is again mere illustration.

The Sun and Moon together also have to do with new beginnings in life, and it means that within the relationship there is the potential if circumstance allow the relationship to strengthen, to make a new beginning, a new life together, if you both have the courage to do so. But the main purpose of the meeting is not about the future but to finish off old karma, an inheritance from the past..

Client's Feed-Back

The client said there had indeed been a death. In the present life too, before she met this man, her favorite grandmother had passed away, a death just as in the past life. She felt the inheritance in the present life was not money, but that her grandmother had left Claire some lace, and a picture, an oil painting, in her will. She had been trying to get some of her grandmother's lace work, and lace making techniques and patterns published or exhibited. (The lace is shown buy Moon in Virgo in eighth house, Virgo is cloth and also crafts rather than arts, the Moon white delicate cloth, the eighth house inheritances, or cloth of the dead) The painting of a man in a dark velvet jacket, ruffled shirt, dining with a lace table cloth, bore at first sight a vague resemble to the modern day man she had met. She'd met Frank at a medieval banquet. (Her ascendant, symbolizing beginnings, in Capricorn conjunct his Saturn, these two, being the past. His Saturn in his second house, house of sustenance, money, food. Food from the past, the banquet. He Sun in Cancer in her seventh house, adding to the symbolism food, cooking homeliness, the old kitchen, and he Jupiter, when linked with food, the planet of the feast, being retrograde ,i.e. the past on his ascendant.) She recalled his black velvet jacket but not much else. She did not know who the portrait was of. The man she had met was a school teacher, a history teacher, who was now helping her trace her family tree. They had become friends. (His chart, Jupiter, opposing his eighth house and his tenth house and eighth house both ruled by mercury, suggest his profession in the past life was, an official or a lawyer, to do with goods or moneys of the dead. Jupiter, who rules the law, the church and the school and who in the present life rules teaching)

Trying to get the lace recognized was something she'd tried to do in her grandmother's life time but not succeeded. It was now her way of honoring her grandmother's memory, or making a gift, an offering to the dead. (In the past life the chart revealed she had benefited from the will of a relative, a gift from the dead you might say, in this life again she had been given something), But the greater gift was the gift of this man, that she had the chance to re-meet him. Symbolized in real life by her grandmothers gift of the picture of a mystery man from the past. She recognized this, synchrony at the time but instinctively felt it was more imperative to find a place to display the lace, she had the notion that if she succeeded in exhibiting the lace perhaps she would succeed in winning this mans love as well as his friendship. Perhaps in this life he would return to her. Her intuition was proved correct.

A few months after he left to take up a position at a Belgium, school, he wrote to invite her to bring some of her grandmother's work, and enquired after the painting. He had made some contacts in a lace making industry there, that he thought might be instrumental in her wish to honor her grandmother. The lace table cloth depicted in the portrait, as well as her grandmother's lace he felt would enhance a display. Her grandmother's lace was exhibited as part of a museum display. A year later she and the man were engaged to be married.

The Karma Explained.

In the past incarnation Franks Career had involved him with legal matters. Family wills and inheritances. A karmic thread woven in the tapestry of time will twist or distort slightly from life to life, but will still be traceable, like a theme. In the present life, Frank's involvement and interest is still with legal documents and families and in tracing ancestries, the family tree. This is his hobby, not his profession in the present life. In both lives this was a "helping karma" to do with Claire's ancestry, but an unfinished one. The karmic task, in both lives was a sacred one to do with the " will " of her ancestors or to put it another way helping fulfill the last desire of a much love deceased person. This same karmic theme was handed down through time from the past incarnation to the present to both of them, each in their different ways and within the theme of their separate lives. Their inner spirit or "higher self " had decided this sacred task of ancestry had to come before their own love. Hence the obstacles, the separation, the slow unfolding of the friendship, that made Claire doubt if there was any future. The future could only come after the completion of the past.

Frank's Luna nodes are over his career axis. So his career, he is a history teacher in this life, or his life's work which is in family trees, and old records, archives is a karmic line of fate generally in his life. Even if he'd never met Claire his career or life's work would have been karmic. The nodes in his chart conjunct with Claire's house of ancestry, this is where his karma, or karmic career connects with her life.

This house is also the house of debts, karmic debts; it suggests he owed her ancestor a debt of work. We don't know why exactly, perhaps Claire's family in the past life had helped him in business, in money, or had in some way furthered his law prospects. His higher spirit wanted to repay this debt, and be free of it and felt it had to be repaid before he could realize and accept Claire's love. Claire with her intuitive eighth house Moon was more conscious of the task handed down to her, than Frank, whose chart is not so intuitive. Once this karmic task was settled, the two were free to build their new life together, this would have felt like karmic reward, but was really just the resolution of old karma, so new karma could begin and the relationship move on from the past. The picture she inherited was not a picture of Frank in his past life, through there may have been something reminiscent of that, but it was a kind of symbolic karma, an image, an unknown but attractive man from the past, someone unknown who'd always been with her, who would come into her life.. The two charts have many cross aspects indicating that they are indeed Soulmates

The north and south node are always opposite each other and they work like an axis. Both are karmic. Some astrologers believe the South node is the past life and what we are moving away from in our karma. The north node what we are taking into the future or present life from the past life. My own researches show it is not as clear cut as that. The south node doesn't always mean what we are leaving behind. In Franks chart it is his north node reconnecting with Claire's house of death and reincarnation, showing the karma being brought forwards.

Definitions

Here is a list of definitions, for the houses with special emphasis on what they mean in the soulmate relationship. They have lots of other definitions and meanings in general astrology, but here we concentrate only on soulmate relationships in this book.

Houses

1st 4th 7th 10th are the houses of the Present incarnation. The soulmate and our life and relationship with him.

The 2nd 5th 8th 11th, the mutual karmic tasks to be completed, tasks that belong to the soulmate relationship.

The 3rd 6th 9th $12^{th,}$ the past incarnation of the soulmate, and past life karma of the soulmate relationship.

In a synastry reading where two charts link together (as Frank and Claire's did) it shows at a glance something of the karmic connections. Frank's nodes conjuncting Claire's eighth house. The mutual task to be completed. His Nodes in his radix being 10th house, present life career, connected with past life karma, and so on. In Claire's own chart the ruler of her house of soulmates, and her Venus, are in the eighth house. Before ever she had met frank if she could read this in astrology, she knew there was mutual karmic task to be completed with her future soulmate..

The purpose of a karmic interpretation, is to give an insight into the present. So that we can understand ourselves and the pattern our life has made, through time. To know a past life can be to find an unknown part of the self, it can be a magical thing, which is startling and profoundly personal, and has to be experienced because its emotion and inner feeling cannot be conveyed in any other way. It can make unexplained pieces of your life fall into place.

There would be no point in a Karma reading only giving people a long list of lives, i.e. "You were a dancer in one life, a prostitute in another, a ship's captain in another etc.", it would have no meaning or relevance. A karma reading only has meaning in how the past life pattern fits with the present incarnation. It has relevance in that it confirms as Claries reading did, that she'd known Frank before this life, that their love was old and ongoing., that's why the feelings were so inexplicable and special. When a karma reading confirming this, it also means you will meet again in a future life, this can be comforting if the one you love has been irretrievably lost, or has passed on from this mortal life, leaving you to struggle alone with only memories and cares like falling leafs.

Never hasten a reunion, if you're left alone, it is also for a karmic purpose that you must continue. If you work to improve or complete your own karma., the karmic reading will guide you in ways to do it.

The Luminaries - Moon

The Problem Corner

A person with the Moon in the seventh house wrestles with a difficult karma. If you have the Moon in this house, you have almost certainly met your marriage partner or soulmate in a past incarnation, but in that past incarnation you may have been children. Or one may have been a child and the other an adult.

The Moon which is a symbol of infancy, the mother, the mother's milk, the cradle of the past. The past self, immaturity, the home and family, the emotional part of the character. The Moon is nurturing, nostalgia, and dependency; the Moon is always pulling us back to the past in hidden ways and in other subtler ways drawing things back that we should have left behind. This can be negative and disturbing or positive influence. Most likely or a mingling of both, like all the celestial bodies.

The negative things arising from the past and carried forwards include the insecurities, and instabilities inside of us. Past life karma, and uncertainty, feelings and frustration that are like an echo of those from childhood.

A person with the Moon in the seventh house needs to look deeply at their own character and own emotional needs. For sooner or later they will be made to confront these through the seventh house of the chart, through the soulmate relationship or in marriage. The closer to the seventh cusp the more troubled an upsetting the relationship can be.

Moon and immaturity.

The Child Bride - The Moon rules infancy and childhood. When there is a troubled relationship and a seventh house Moon appearing, in the synastry, or in the persons own radix chart one possible cause of the misery can be immaturity in the self or in the marriage partner, the archetype of the " child bride", or " Mother Boy. ". If you are the child bride, you may have to learn hard karmic lessons, through marriage, about material self sufficiency. If you seek a marriage where you are provided for, indulged and kept, where you are protected and have all troubles and responsibilities and difficult circumstances averted before they begin effect you, Then you are looking for a parent, not a partner, and the fate of the marriage will be like a thorny path that teaches you hard lessons about self sufficiency, through which you will eventually mature. By acknowledging this situation and attempting to mature inwardly, you will find strength and independence, you will emerge as a strong responsible woman or man capable of standing on your own feet and taking an equal role, not a child.

This scenario is more common with the Moon in the seventh in the earth signs. It can also be a theme of the Luna nodes in the seventh house in earth sign.

The Married Bachelor.

If the man or woman you love acts as though they are still single. The seventh house Moon is still about immaturity. This is not the cradled infant who expects to be kept. He or she may be a materially successful, generous and responsible. This is the adolescent, who did not grow on to maturity. He or she doesn't like to be tied down, thinks of sexual encounters and love affairs as a game, Has his own social life, his freedom which is much as it was when he was a single man..

The seventh house Moon in an Air or fire sign, can result in this scenario, intellectual immaturity, lack of commitment, and rashness and irresponsibility

The Mother's Boy

Some times if you have the Moon in the seventh house, you feel that you may as well have married the man's mother or family, not the man. That they have too much influence either directly or indirectly over you partners life. If he has not made the full transition from son to husband and father, part of him is still a child. If you are both to be happy in the marriage the karmic task is in making him mature, so that like his own father, he finally come to put his wife and children first. This becomes easier to achieve when you see through the emotional fog of anger and despair that surrounds the rocky times and rows in the marriage, and realize with clarity that his behavior is only that of a little child. Like a child you must help him leave behind his childish things and emotionally grow into the adult within him. The adult you fell in love with, before you knew he had not emotionally separated himself from his family..

The element the Moon occupies may give another clue as to in what way partner (or self) has not fully grown up. In a water element, the person is emotionally immature.

The Mothers boy scenario is often the seventh house Moon in a water sign. The seventh house Moon in Libra, usually works positively and gives a happy peaceful marriage. It can also work well in Cancer, the family sign.

Needs of the Moon.

Having looked at the general possibility of immaturity, and it remains only a possibility outlined by a seventh house Moon, because much depends on if the Moon or the seventh house is afflicted and badly aspected, We can never make a judgment on one planet's position alone. But then we can look at the Moons subconscious message, the Moon is a needy planet. It can reveal what you most need or subconsciously seek in a marriage or lasting involvement. This need is strong when the Moon is in the seventh house..

As an example someone with the Moon here and in Taurus may have an overpowering but subconscious need for material or emotional security. The reason for marriage and choice of partner will be based around that need. So it will begin quite well but if the relationship does not continue to provide that security then it can become stormy, difficult and unhappy. If the need is for material security rather than emotional and the partner loses his livelihood then the marriage may flounder, not from misfortune or lack of money but because of the distress from insecurity of a lost job or an irregular income.

If emotional security is the problem, in the Taurus seventh house Moon then a crushing possessiveness and scalding jealousy may result, and continually spoil the happiness of the love relationship. With the Moon one has to ask the question is the jealousy rational, or irrational and unnecessarily. In either case, it's a hard journey and even if the marriage does succeed, it will at some stage go down the unstable corridors before peace and true security is arrived at. In a genuine soulmate relationship coping with troubles will always strengthen and mature the character, it won't break the essential unity.

To a lesser extent if your Moon is not in the seventh but aspecting the seventh house Taurus, your life with have weaker watered down traces of the same pattern stamped on it, but much paler. An example is was a client with a fourth house Moon, aspecting the cusp of seventh house Taurus, and the instability was not in the marriage, which was her rock and strength, but in the home, in the first eight years of marriage she moved house six times. This was daunting but not upsetting and did not affect the overall happiness of her marriage.

The Luminaries - Sun

The Sun of Independence

The Moon in karmic astrology is a symbol the past life self. The Moon is what we were born, in this incarnation, it is our infant self our emotions, our instincts. As children we resemble our Moon sign more than our Sun sign. The Sun is what we become. The Sun is the future that we move towards each day that passes. As we grow older and the character becomes better defined, the traits of our Sun sign crystallize. The Moon is immaturity, past karmas we are still working on; the Sun is maturity, advancement. In astrology the Sun has always been regarded as a symbol of the self. This is because is reminiscent of the light, the spark of pure spirit burning within that creates the life force. The solar system, our world, revolves round the Sun, and in this incarnation our perception of our own individual life or own world, its events and people, its love and losses, joys and sorrows, is also experienced with us in the centre. The blanket of experiences wrapped like a cocoon around our eternal core of light, and extending to the edges of our perception. The Sun is important. If the Sun is the self, it also contains something of our soulmate, our anima, our twin spirit and much more.

A woman with the Sun on this house will not be contented to be oppressed in marriage, she will want a life with a wider outlook. She will expect more form life than mere marriage and will want some kind of recognition for her talent or success in the work place. For this reason it is sometimes difficult for such people to find love. Though when it finally comes it is happy. The seventh house Sun person may also find they are the dominant partner in the marriage. In a man's case he will absorb himself I the marriage.. In a woman's case the reverse may happen and she may take on the traditional masculine role of the marriage. She may be the one with the career. The decision maker. The Sun is beginnings, so in a sense with the Sun in the seventh house the person always begins a new life after marriage.

The Sun aspecting the seventh from any other part of the chart has a similar but diluted effect. The exception to this astrological rule, is when the Sun is in Cancer, the natural sign of the family and homemaker. A woman with Sun in Cancer on the seventh, will be happy to make the family and family concern, children, housekeeping, family business, maintain ties with the wider relatives and in-laws her life's work, but will also be matriarch of it eventually.

If the Sun is in an earth sign, the independence sought or fated within marriage is usually material, that of money possessions, work., the independence to earn ones own living, or to have ones own financial allowance. A woman with Capricorn Sun here will marry not only her husband but his job. She may take an interest in his job or a supporting role, but she will have independence and equality as well.

If in water signs, emotional independence is required. If fire, an independent social life, independent activities, and life style after the marriage, while still being united and happy. If Air, independent ambitions will be pursued.

Ancient astrology books would dismally state that the Sun in the seventh house has a greater tendency not to marry, and less chance of finding any love. The Sun is a symbol of the self, and the seventh house means they are married to the self. That there is no room for anyone else in their life or ego. Or that they have evolved beyond marriage and are happy alone. Times must have changed and what was perhaps once true is no longer so true. In past times a marriage was expected to be dependency. The Sun is an independent planet but I have fond that to most people with a seventh house Sun, relationships, settling down and finding the true soulmate are of the utmost importance. They want another self, to centre their world around, and rebuild their life but without losing their individuality, they want an equal partnership, or an evolved one for the modern times in which we live. Usually they find it and are the happiest of people.

If you have the Sun in the seventh house, you may want to find a twin soul, or a clone, another self, yes, but ideally you should look instead for some one, who is the kind of person you would *like* to become. The kind of person you aspire to be, this is the karma you are heading towards now.

When Will I Meet My Soulmate?

When will love wake your soul from winter and take away the infinite loneliness of existence? All things are interconnected For example clients usually only write to me for a soulmate chart at a time in their lives when they have without knowing entered the era in which they will find their ultimate love. It is as though the inner self has unknowingly guided them to me, to be shown a glimpse through the door of time

People like to be given exact dates, but as to when the meeting of soulmates will take place, there is clock time and karmic time. The clock time is the easier to estimate but is less accurate. We work this out from the astrology chart, it's an individual calculation. For some people it is correct and exact for other it is wide of the mark.

From your chart I can only make an estimate. The fate that really determines time is karmic, not cosmic, that is to say various events that will shape your life and character have to happen first before you can meet . These events are usually ones which will cause inner psychological or karmic change. The alchemy of experience that changes us all and makes us into the person we are today, instead of the person we used to be.

Then when this inner change, change in understanding has taken place you meet

Each person's karma goes at its own pace, Karma can delay or speed a thing up . In theory you can hasten the meeting, if you find the way to become the person you are destined to be sooner. The inner self is, or subconscious is very powerful, it knows when you meet this love will, and it knows what it has to do to evolve. The outer self obstructs, gets caught in the tangle of life like a fish in a net unable to swim further. When a person doesn't meet their soulmate, at the estimated time they should, or if they meet him earlier or later. It means that in relationship may really be based in karmic time.

Karmic time is not easy to estimate, and can usually only be given accurately as a series of events, saying "after this and that has happened" as each person's karma goes at its own pace Clock time and Karmic time sometimes tie up, sometimes not, the Karma time can delay or speed it up.

When it speeds things up and the soulmate arrives early, there is no great problem, only joy, though I have found in some cases meeting him sooner can slow the relationship so that the courtship is longer or conditions to love or marry are not quite right at the time of the meeting, though in most cases everything speeds up. It is karmic delays that are a great cause of anguish and agony. (Always if it hasn't worked out have your chart checked, error is human. If no-fault shows, or no other explanation then it is love that's held back on the other side of time, but you can bring it forwards by or unlocking the karma, or working on the inner self.

There many reasons why love is withheld, most are complicated, but rest assured it is never withheld for ever. Your soulmate will come to you.

Soulmate relationship are usually karmic, and the long term experience of them is also often like a new life a rebirth a time a love that transforms ones life. It can do so instantly or over a period of time.

Now some interesting charts to illustrate how soulmate astrology can help answer those haunting questions.

What became of the missing ring?

The chart is that of a man of Indian ancestry called Amadeep. He was born in England. In December 2002. He broke off an engagement with Romash, and requested his gifts back, including a ring, that he had given her. He then left the country without further explanation. Romash wanted to know, what became of

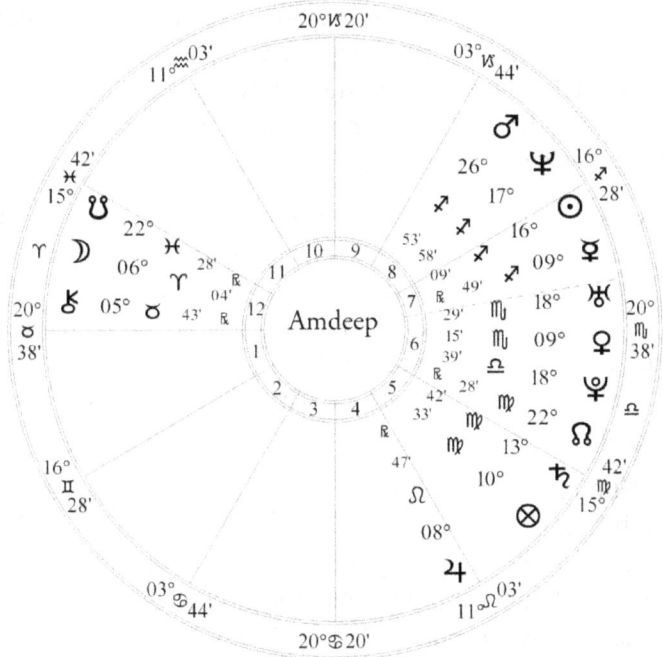

her gold bangle, and a turquoise and sapphire ring. Did he give them to another woman.?.

In December 2002 in Amadeep's chart Transit Pluto, the planet of endings and beginnings and the ruling planet of his house of marriage and engagements was conjunct to Natal Neptune on the cusp of his eighth house, showing the end of the engagement, a long journey and the beginning of a new life in a country that was foreign to him but which he felt drawn to.

There is nothing to suggest another woman. The eighth house is the house of death and reincarnation and wealth. This suggests he may have sold or pawned the ring for money. Pluto suggests there are some hidden financial difficulties in his life. Some drain on his income. Selling the ring was a way of solving this. This is why he asked for it back. Transit Mercury was also conjoined with Pluto and Neptune at the time. Mercury rules the fingers. Just as by reflex on the opposite house Gemini rules the hands or wrist. The ring and the bangle.

He was a boy from a wealthy family, and Romash had the jewelry valued. It was his handsome face and his family's wealth that had induced her to accept the offer of marriage. Astrologically we know both have a financial value too because this is the house of money, not the house of decoration. Amadeep's Sun is also on the cusp.

The Sun rules the metal gold, (and brass) but because it is eighth house or wealth it is more inclined to be gold so we get the picture of the gold ring and bangle. Pluto rules anything that is mined. The turquoise astrologically belongs to December, ruled by Sagittarius, the sign on Amadeep's eighth cusp. This also rules other blue stones.

Pluto Neptune aspect on this house also has to do with mysterious disappearances, missing persons and deaths..

In this case Amadeep left the both the country, and the mystery of why he'd broken off his engagement behind him. Did he meet a premature death? (Neptune and transit Pluto in the house of death). Or was it a new life that felt like a death and rebirth. Romash said his life was like a closed book to her. He was cruel arrogant and changeable. She suspected an involvement in drug dealing (Neptune), but she knew nothing for certain.

The demand for the jewelry suggests premeditate intention to leave, rather than a haphazard encounter with misadventure. Transit Jupiter, the ruler of his house of death and which is his own ruling planet had completed a return*, in his fourth house, the house of the home and home land, two months earlier, showing the end of a phaze in his life.

Transit Jupiter was not so badly afflicted. He was in Leo, the suns own sign. A mutual reception, because in December the Sun is in Sagittarius. He was in trine to the transit Pluto and his own Sun and Neptune, and Jupiter was his ruling planet. Ones ruler rarely brings a catastrophic fate, and Jupiter is a fortunate planet. Though there are exceptions.

The eighth house is the house of ancestry and heritage as well as the house of death, so this more suggest an intention of a journey, due to an opportunity he had been offered (Jupiter) to India the land of his forebears.

---

* A 'Return' is when a planet has traveled full circle around the zodiac and come back to its Natal place in the chart. Such a return means the completion of a cycle. A Jupiter return takes twelve years to happen, so it is of significance.

The curiosity shop

I have called this chapter the curiosity shop, because that is what it is. You will find displayed a few peculiar or interesting charts, show cased as if in a shop window, for your perusal. The charts are from my much treasured private collection and as samples they do not really belong in any one category of the soul mate book they are too uncommon but they are not simply a museum exhibit for the morbidly curious. Odd as these cases are you will learn something unique from each and every example; I have provided short explanations, after that you are left to muse or pore over them yourself.

All the charts have to do with unusual lives or loves. We see the chart of a handsome, ordinary, confident man who seems to have much offer a soul mate both emotionally and materially but has never had a relationship in his entire life, not even an unrequited one, or a fleeting attraction, or a romantic date. We see a chart where a certain time of year seems tragically fatalistic. A marriage that lasted an hour or so, and a most unusual meeting place, where soul mate met soul mate.

There is nothing as strange as fate or love.

Lightening strikes twice;

The chart reproduced here is that of a woman. Jayne said "My husband left me on the night between the years – My brother died 31/12/99 at this same, new year-old year time".

The time between years was often a fatalistic time for Jayne, not always deaths, but a times of revelation, as if the old year-new year was a portal, when she'd find out some shattering truth, or some great change. You will see the melancholy transit of Saturn, planet of death and endings approaching Jayne's eighth house cusp and opposing her Sun. Saturn co- ruler of her third house the house of siblings.

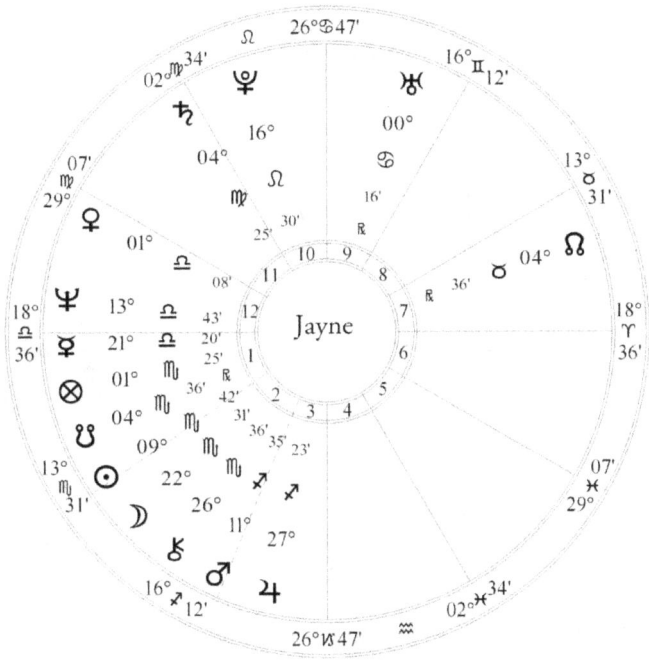

Also transit Pluto at this time conjuncting Mars ruler of her seventh. There are other aspects to be observed in this chart, but I shall leave that for you to find..

Love Delayed

This chart is of a man who wrote to me for a soulmate reading when he was aged 45.

In his short letter James said " I have never been married or had a meaningful relationship of any kind. " Being a student of astrology he also added he thought , that it

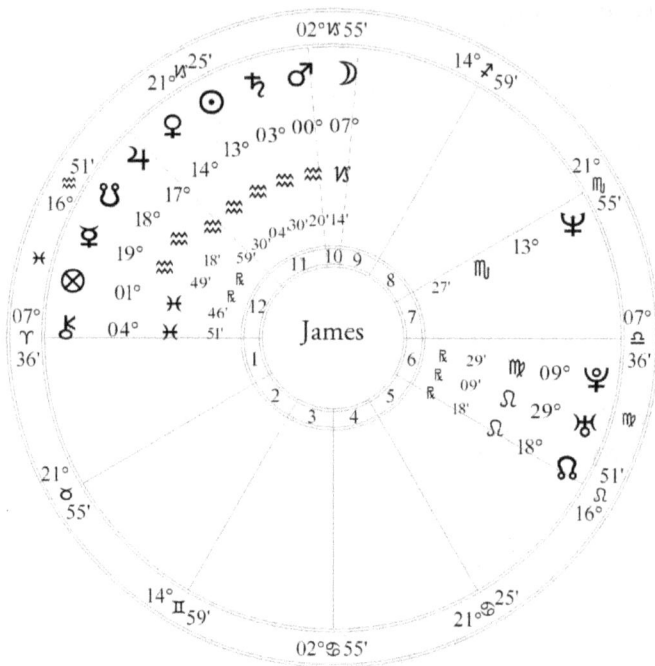

was because he had Neptune in the seventh house.

James chart has several "afflictions". Venus, the planet of love and ruler of his house of marriage, is conjunct the cusp of his twelfth house. This shows difficulties in relationships Mercury is also retrograde, it makes it harder for him to communicate. Venus touching this house shows a greater potential for clandestine relationships, in James case unrequited dreams of love, since Neptune aspect Venus from his seventh house.

James confessed to writing anonymous love letters to strangers he became enamored with. The square between Neptune and the retrograde Mercury .Venus conjuncts his Sun. The Sun is the self and Venus brings try's to bring love into his life, but his ruling planet Uranus is retrograde, This delays , both Venus's promise of love, and the Sun, and so has held back many other things in James life too.

Jupiter in the midst of these planets expands on the difficulties, and does little to help. Libra is considered strong, because it's the natural ruler of the seventh house but not so the rest of the seventh house which occupied by Scorpio. Pluto Scorpios ruler, and the co ruler of his marriage house, the planet capable of transforming it all, is also retrograde. There will be much delay before James very suddenly finds his love..

Famous Travels

Helena Petrovna Blavatsky; Founder of the Theosophical Society. Born Ekaterinaslav, Ukraine, on the night between midnight 30th July to 31st before sunrise next day. In Alan Leo's the book, 1001 Notable Nativities, he quotes a chart for Madam Blavatsky with MC at 17 Pisces, and Ascendant at Cancer 13. This is technically not possible to draw up by computer, in those days charts were calculated by hand. So I have reproduced the chart as closely as I can with one degree difference. Madam Blavatsky's chart is of interest because, a marriage of convenience was entered into when she was aged seventeen. Not unusual for those days I would have thought.

The strange thing is she deserted her husband on the

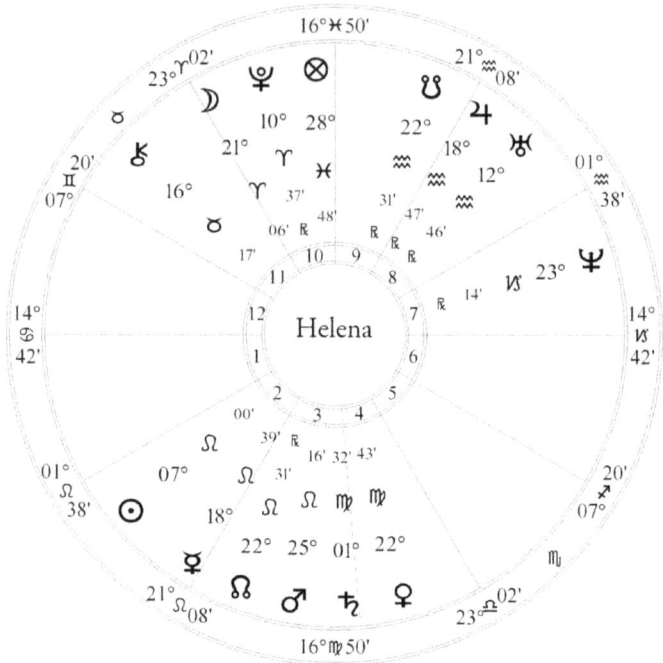

day of her marriage, and traveled for a time of ten years. On her chart you will see the Neptune in the seventh house, aspecting the Moon, and the difficult Mars and Venus aspects to Moon and Neptune.

Pat and the Biker

The next chart is another from my own chart archives. Pat, a colorful strong willed outgoing character, was born with a withered leg that she had amputated. She met a new boyfriend, a biker much younger than herself whose painted jacket, rugged face and gentle manner she admired, and after a short time dating they were living together happily. The curious thing is, he also had only one leg !

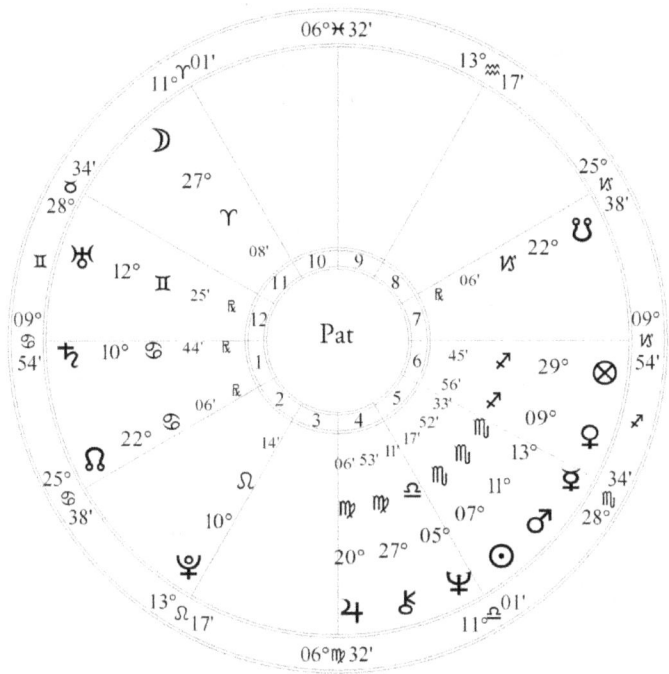

He lost his leg in a motor bike accident. Amazing coincidence, or a true soulmate destiny? They actually met at a clinic where Pat was having a new artificial limb fitted. The relationship broke up after six years. I don't know if there was a reconciliation, but soulmates, maybe. Pat a spiritual healer said her task was to show him hope that life doesn't end, when you think it has. I leave her chart for your perusal.

The Gay life

This unusual chart of a lady whom I have called Miki. She has known her soulmate for many years now, she feels she will know him until the end of their lives, they are spiritually close and he is a wonderful devoted man, but he is a homosexual. Miki loves him with all her heart. When the man thought that Miki might leave Japan forever, he could not bare the pain of it, he gets jealous when she dates other men.

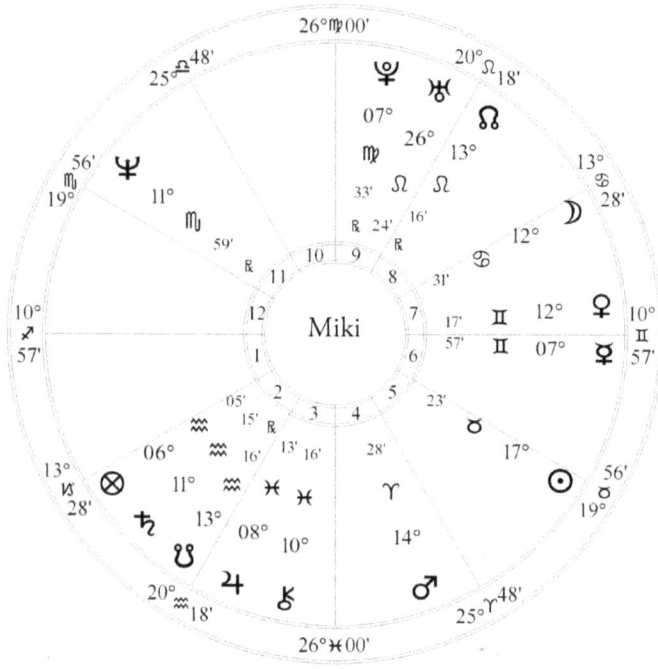

Miki says I probably do not love him passionately but at a much deeper level we understand each other instantly. But him being gay we are never sexually attached, is this our karmic fate I wonder? It is hard for me, is this my fate, I have to accept it, and face it?

If your knowledge of astrology is a little advanced you may note the Yod. This unusual astrological formation in her chart is also known as the "Finger of Fate" and is a

Y shaped star formation, it is very difficult and fatalistic to live through. It is a stress aspect formed by two planets sixty degrees apart and a third that is quincunx to the two, like a y shape.

In Miki's chart the Yod is composed of Saturn and Neptune in square to each other and in quincunx to the seventh house and the planet of the seventh house cusp, Venus, and mercury.

The finger of fate is like the line of force on a building, or the stitches in the seam on a garment, it is the place in the mind where if enough psychological pressure is applied, your life will start to tear apart at the seams and you'll break down. And this is eventually what happened.

The Yod is like a crack on a wall it cannot be seem at first until it begins to slowly open up when the pressure of various events in life pull heavily. And this is a slow aspect not a sudden one. It can begin with a simple emotion like say betrayal or a simple event, but there is always so much more behind it that the wound that is done to you often cannot be put into words.

The finger of fate always occurs at a time that will lead up to great emotional pressure and stress. Usually there is more than one event causes this, it can be an ongoing situation that gets continually harder and harder to face, but equally impossible to escape from.

Love and death.

Emily Bronte, the most romantic of northern writers was the daughter of an Irish born parson. She lived in Yorkshire, in the imposing stone house that is known as

Haworth Parsonage. She and the entire family, with the exception of her sister Anne, lie buried in a vault covered in concrete at the foot of one of the pillars which forms the entrance to the present church.

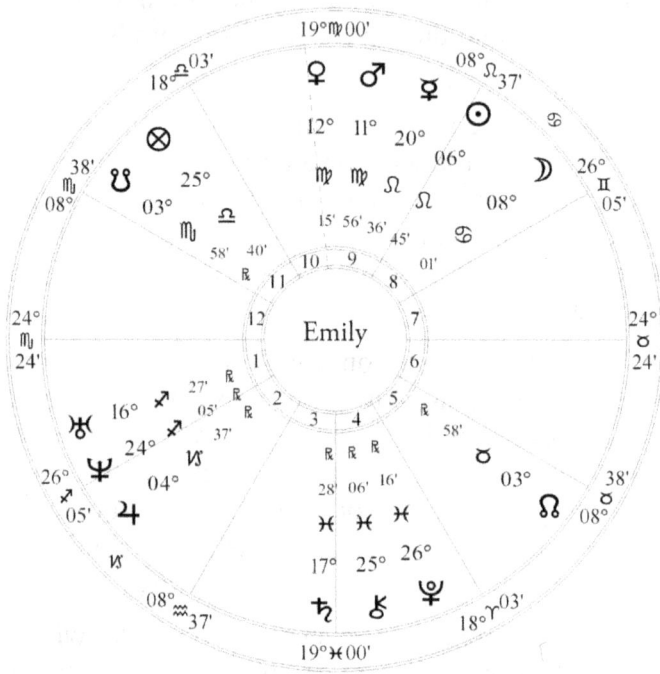

Haworth is bleak in winter and scenic in summer, a staggering stone village with a cobbled road that rises up to the heights, set in the midst of the Yorkshire moors. Emily wrote of Haworth Parsonage, of the dank moss dripping from the wall, the mute bird sitting on the stone, the over grown weeds.

In her chart Saturn conjuncting the forth house cusp in Pisces reflects this image she had of the damp austere parsonage, dank moss, stone built, timeless and limiting, even the neglect of weeds, are all Saturn images. Saturn is cold gloomy, desolate, while Pisces is damp, religious. Pisces is the last zodiac sign and Saturn is mortality, endings. A place of death and endings then for Emily. A house full of shadows. Saturn, like Jupiter, Pisces co ruler can symbolize the father. The "Fathers house". A church. A parsonage, both very Saturn in Pisces. Tradition and religion.

Wuthering heights, her book, can be seen here too in the concealed images, Wuthering means "Sobbing Heights". Again the Saturn cusp, Saturn is sorrows, Pisces being water, is tears, weeping sorrows, and placed fractionally in the third house in its conjunction, the third is literature, communication, ones written works.

This may seem like making details fit in a contrived way. But in life every detail does fit with your chart, just as every detail of your face fits with your reflection in a mirror. We cannot always find the fit because our knowledge is limited, but it is all there. The astrology chart is the book of your life. With the Sun in Leo, Emily had the potential to be more extrovert in character than she was. But in the eighth house the Sun is overshadowed by death and somberness. Her Moon, in Cancer, also in the eighth house, shows a great attachment to family, but her mother, two sisters and her brother all died before her.

It's hardly any wonder that her writings were full of death and love, and ghosts and beautiful but morbid things, when her own life was filled with grief and endings. Here is a verse from her poem "Remembrance", again a Saturn theme.

No other Sun has lightened up my heaven;
No other star has ever shone for me;
All my life's bliss from thy dear life was given –
All my life's bliss is in the grave with thee.

Emily's book "Wuthering Heights" is one of the greatest soulmate stories, and gothic novels in English literature. This would be justification alone for including her chart in my soulmate book, without any other reason, but Emily is also an interesting figure, reclusive and solitary. The book was published in 1847. Then sadly the following winter of 1848 almost as if her task on this Earth was done, Emily became ill, she grew steadily worse, but refused all medication that may have helped her, and she died in the same parsonage where she had lived. Emily was never married. There is no record of her ever having had a love affair. So what does her chart show of soulmates, or of a loneliness wider than the moors, a life that was as short and brilliant as a shooting star, and her work that is an immortal shrine to her existence. How could someone write a book like Wuthering Heights and know nothing of life or love?

The chart has a curious aspect that may suggest a love hidden from the world, when Emily was in her early twenties (Neptune, unrequited love, broken promises, dreams and illusions, far off places). That the person may have died, precluding any chance of a future. Or he may never have lived, except in her mind like an enduring dream or a companion created out of loneliness. Sometimes a dream is more real than life itself.

Emily would have had admirers, as any single girl in a small country village would. Even if she shunned them. Venus, planet of love and ruler of her seventh house, aspects Saturn at a wide weak orb. The chart suggests an older man. He lived not far away (Saturn in fourth) but Saturn in Pisces would suggest he was an emotionally isolated man,. Had personal difficulties, fearfulness, neurosis, inclined to live in the past not in the present. Difficult coping with the present and the modern world. Reclusive or confined to his home. Shy serious and depressed.. Saturn is stone, Pisces is a damp dark cold stone house, near water, a brooks, stream or ditch that was attractive. This man would be rather closed and shy in personality. Possibly a widower.

In appearance tall, dark almost black hair the Neptune aspects make him slightly foreign in looks, and disheveled, a hard boned face, straight hair, a tendency to bow the head when walking and avoid eye contact, gaunt. Long shabby coat. The feet gave him trouble. A love that was never spoken. Unfulfilled love and financial hardships that made it impossible. Saturn is retrograde, so it's a love that is held back. The man may have been just an image, a figure that inspired her. A love that could have happened but didn't, their paths would have crossed but they were both too isolated emotionally to reach out. Too many barriers between them. Too close, too far apart. Both people lived too much in their own world. He in the past, her in her dreams. They were not soulmates as such. More two souls united by loneliness,. They noticed each other, that was all.

Saturn is also inhibitions in love, restrictions Saturn

stifles love, and leaves it unspoken. No one could compete with the unknown love she would conceive of in her early twenties. So the earthly man who ever he was had no chance He is described in her chart that's all, like a path not taken. Remember Emily's Pluto, also retrograde and held back, and Neptune, her longing, she wanted a love that was as great as this memory or dream in her head, that nothing could ever extinguish and which could erase her loneliness and grief forever.. She sought a love that did not exist, sought her soulmate who had either not reincarnated or was already dead, or lost to her. But who lived on in the chambers of her mind..

Retrogrades are also karmic planets (she has five retrogrades in her chart, showing she lived unknowingly, with her soul half steeped in the past incarnation). Retrogrades are the past life, if we turn these aspects inwards instead of outwards, we can say this stranger, (and any other would be lovers) the worldly life, and love was not enough for Emily, because she too in her own way was bound to the past, but to a past incarnation instead, one she could not remember, and a soulmate who appeared only vaguely to her in the guise of her characters and in a make believe, the soulmate of her dreams. Had he, her soulmate lived in this earthly life, she would not have had the gift to reach across the divide, to draw on such a well of solitude and depth and darkness within her, to write such special things, this was her souls purpose.

Emily died of the "White Plague", tuberculosis that caused coughing up blood in the lungs, wasting of the body until she became like a frail ghost and settled in the joints turning them white. Her last hours were spent on the couch in front of the fire, in the parsonage. (Death in her chart shows by the house of death being in Gemini, implicating the lungs, because Gemini rules the lungs, arms hands and wrists. The opposition of Neptune, in medical astrology Neptune is al lingering and wasting and weakening diseases. The ruler of the house of death, mercury being in Leo, (Mercury in medical astrology is joints, Leo the heart) suggests that at some stage in life her heart was probably affected or weakened, by illness, as well her joints perhaps a rheumatic fever; though as far as I am aware there is no record of that..

Neptune aspects the seventh house and the eighth house. So does Pluto. It reveals a subconscious longing for love, and death and transformation. This is not quite the same as a death wish. We cannot know what was in Emily's mind, but perhaps she longed for love that would transform her life, in a way that she had no power to do herself, and then in illness believed death would transform her lonely world, perhaps uniting her with her Soulmate. ?

The ninth house, follows on from the death house, and it shows what fate, if any, follows death; Our Natal chart does not end when we do! Emily was not famous in her own life time, it was not until after her death that she and her literary works became revered. Though she lived long enough to feel the joy of seeing her master work in print. In her ninth house, there is the Mars Venus conjunction and also Mercury. Mercury could be read as a communication beyond the grave, but it is really a symbol of her literary works, living on. That these works were both dark and romantic (Mars-Venus). Wuthering Heights is the story of soulmates Cathy and Heathcliff,

Emily was an inspired writer, (ninth house, spirits, inspiration, genius). That she never found happiness with a soulmate while on earth, plunged her into imagination, a world that was like the dank moors she loved to stride across when she was fit, full of mists and half seen visions, the haunted realm between one world and another, where love can reach out like a wraith. Could her Soulmate have been the source of her inspiration from the life beyond. With her ninth house Mars and Venus we can hope she met him in the after world, just as the characters in her book Cathy and Heathcliff were united in death to haunt the moors.

Emily's birth time was unlikely to be recorded at birth. But whichever astrologer rectified the chart before it in appeared in Kepler's database, seems to have done an excellent job. It wasn't me! Not guilty this time! But it fits beautifully with what's known of her life.

To end I reproduce a verse from her poem; Remembrance.

> And even yet, I dare not let it languish,
>
> Dare not indulge in Memory's rapturous pain;
>
> Once drinking deep of that divinest anguish,
>
> How could I seek the empty world again.

Last words : Soulmates And Lovers

I believe that all deeply felt relationships, have a value. That they should be enjoyed and valued for what they are and what they give to enhance our life. The world is bare place when there is no tapestry of hopes, but we are brought up to think only along the lines of boy meet girl, get engaged, get married or live together, separate or get divorced, meet another. This spoils the enjoyment and intrinsic meaning of life. Not all relationships have to led to marriage, or have taken conventional patterns. Each deep relationship is different, unique, and has its own poetry and own pain and something to enhance our life. It is a rich experience in itself, a flower that grows in the desert. If you can accept a relationship that way, whether it ends or continues, is difficult or easy then this enchantment will only enhance your life and give you something precious, whatever the final outcome; the relationship is a gift as rare and sacred as a to be treasured.

More from Ivarna

The Wisdom Well: a Tarot pack with instructional guide book created by Ivarna Kalinkova, published in 2003, also published as the Wisdom Oracle in 2004.

Ivarna's Soulmate Astrology Volume Two due early 2011.

Astrology services available at www.ivarna.com

Refs & Suggested reading;

The collected works of C.G Jung. Volume 7. Two essays on Analytical Psychology. Anima and Animus; for further information for those interested in psychology.

Wuthering Heights; Emily Bronte.

Birth data used in this work if not from my own records were drawn from Kepler or SolarFire files of Famous people. Those from my own records are genuine but the names have been changed to protect the privacy of the individuals concerned.

Your birth chart can be obtained online from a number of sources including www.zaytsev.com

Recommended software
Zet 9 Geo, top class astrological processing, from www.zaytsev.com
Kepler v7, for birth charts and astrological data; www.AstroSoftware.com
Esoteric Technologies SolarFire; http://alabe.com
Micrografx Picture Publisher; www.micrografx.com.
Microsoft Office; www.microsoft.com

www.ingramcontent.com/pod-product-compliance
Lightning Source LLC
Chambersburg PA
CBHW061951070426
42450CB00007BA/1205